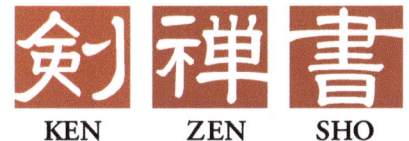

THE ZEN CALLIGRAPHY AND PAINTING OF

YAMAOKA TESSHŪ

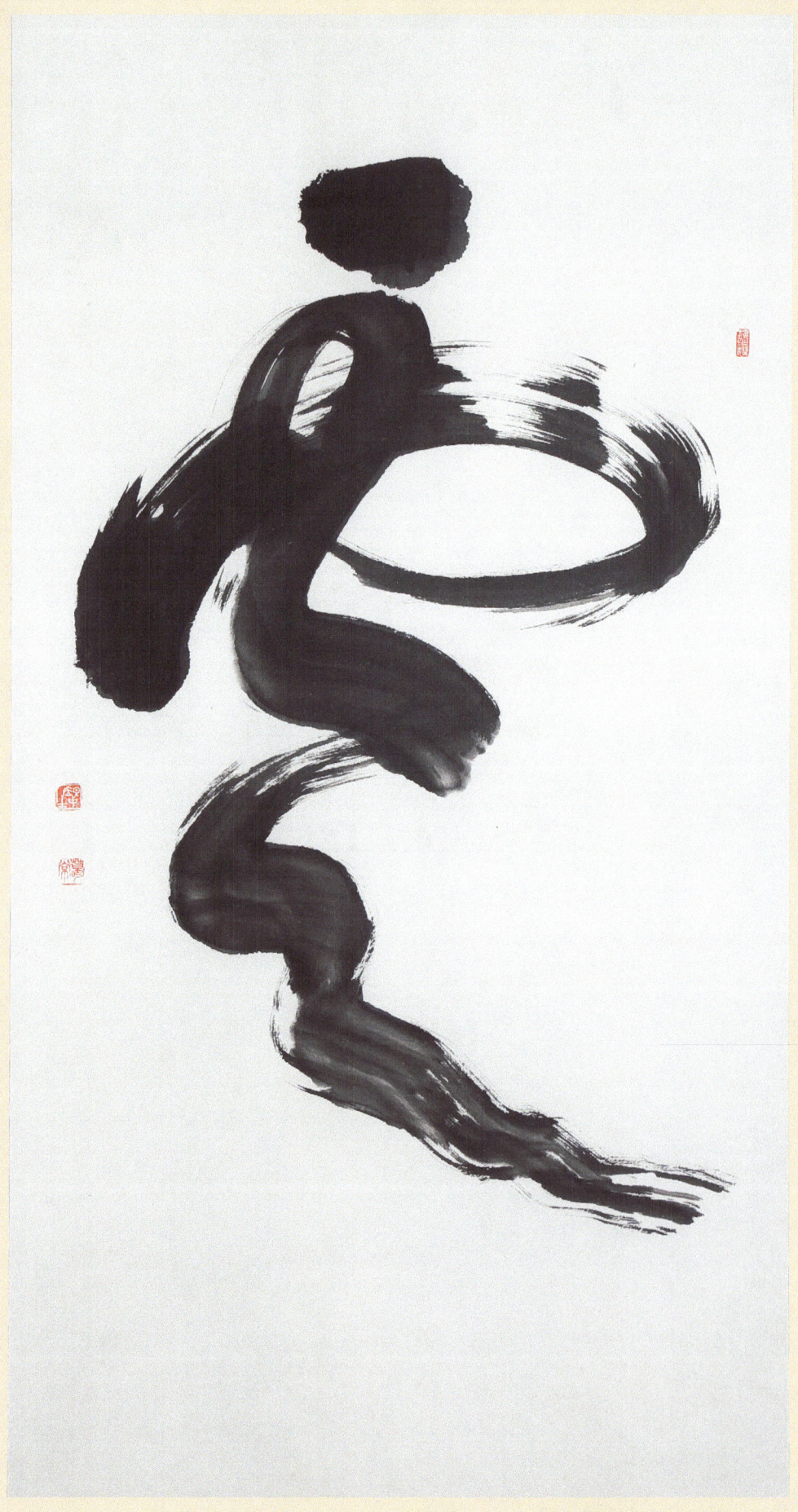

This book is dedicated to the memory of Professor Terayama Tanchū (1938-2007)

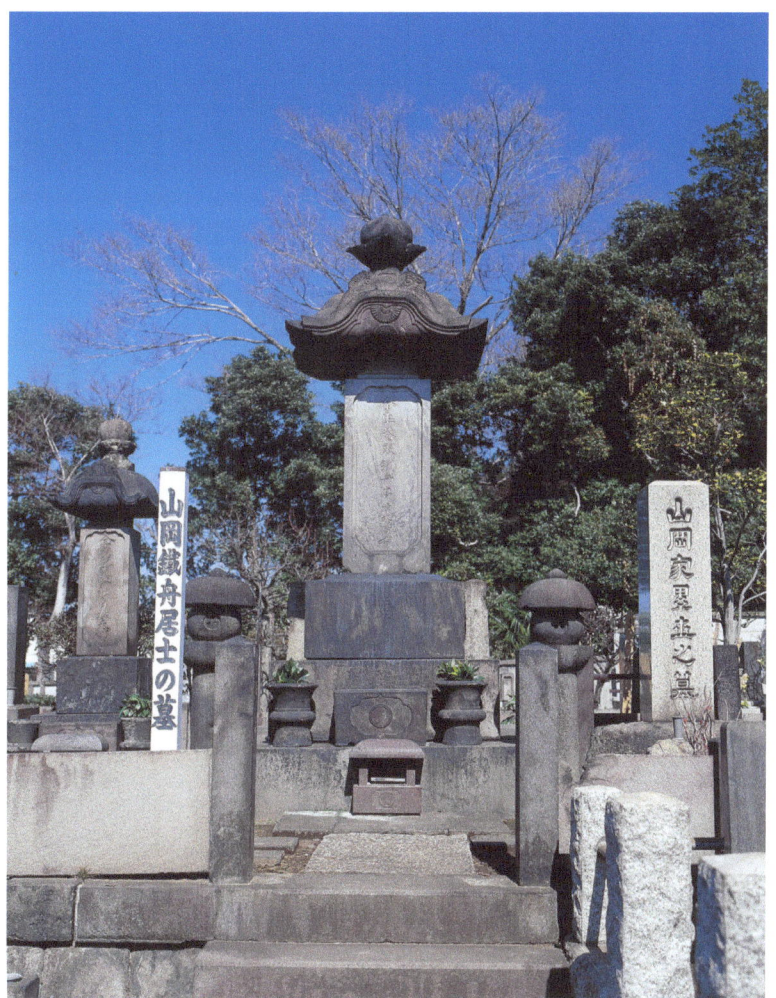

The grave of Yamaoka Tesshū (1836–1888)

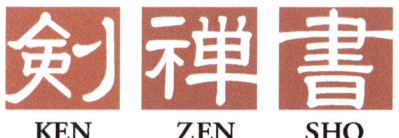

KEN   ZEN   SHO

The Zen Calligraphy and Painting of
YAMAOKA TESSHŪ

Published by Bunkasha International Corporation

Tokyo, Japan

(Editors: Alex Bennett, Sarah Moate)

ISBN 978-4-907009-08-3

First Edition, 2008

CONTENTS

ACKNOWLEDGEMENTS

Bunkasha International would like to thank Professor Terayama Tanchū (1938-2007) without whom this publication would not have been possible, and his wife Mrs. Terayama Yō, who gave kind permission to print the photographs and her husband's essay. Also thanks to Shōshu Hirai, Abbot of Zenshōan in Tokyo for kind permission to print photographs of calligraphy from Zenshōan's extensive collection. We are also indebted to Professor Kubota Noriko, Mrs. Okamura-Bekku Mihoko, Mr. Itō Koshu, Mr. Yokota Hiroatsu for making comments on the text, and also to Professor Uozumi Takashi for his expert guidance in reading *kanbun* (Chinese script). Special thanks go also to Dr. Rupert Faulkner and Professor Takemura Eiji for their unstinting support of this project, and also to the Meiji Tosho Publishing Company in Tokyo, Japan, for permission to print a revised version of Professor Terayama's essay on *ken-zen-sho*.

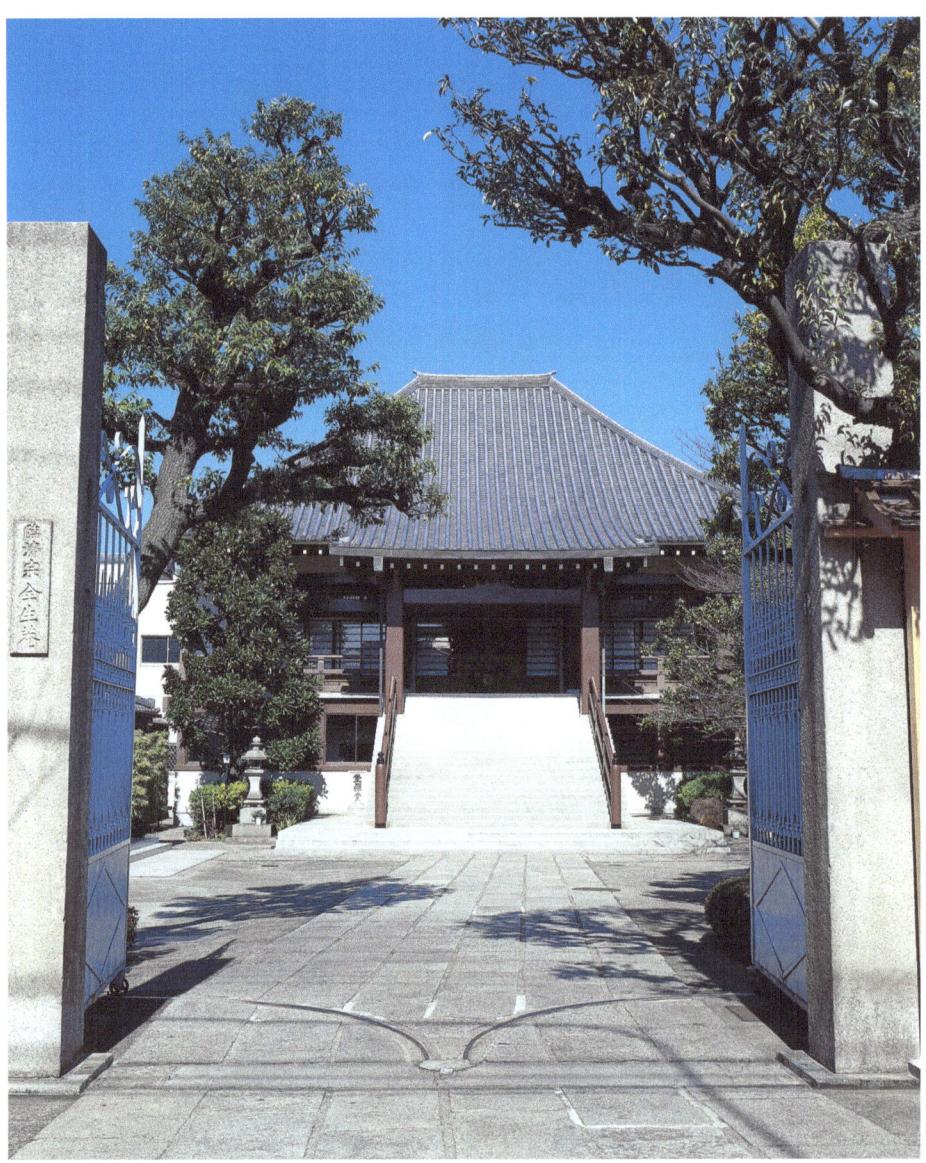

Zenshōan

FOREWORD

The exhibition and demonstration programme taking place at the V&A this autumn were conceived during Terayama-sensei's lifetime as a tribute to Yamaoka Tesshū on the 120th anniversary of his death. But with Terayama-sensei no longer with us, I also think of it as a memorial to him. I know, though, that he wouldn't have wanted anyone to be mawkish about his death, so the image I try to remember him by is the photograph I have of him during the last time I had dinner at his house, some months after he had been diagnosed with cancer. Although thinner than when I had last seen him, he was positively glowing with pleasure at Yō-san's feast and at the enjoyment of entertaining friends from afar.

Ken-zen-sho are three disciplines about which I have little true comprehension, however much I am told or read about them. I think my mind must be too pedestrian to make the leaps of understanding necessary, and not being a practitioner of any kind, I have not benefited from the insights that direct engagement brings. This being said, the numerous meetings I had with the late Terayama-sensei over the course of nearly ten years put paid to any scepticism I might have had about the authenticity of the quest in which he was involved, and which continues to be pursued by his many followers.

On my first visit to Terayama-sensei's house, he, his wife Yō-san, and Sarah Moate, his English student and disciple, demonstrated to me the principles of *yōkihō* through an abbreviated sequence of exercises. I couldn't believe that a man of his age could be so incredibly fit and supple, and I was fascinated to learn how he had invented *yōkihō* by bringing together different elements from a variety of yogic and martial art practices. After the *yōkihō* demonstration we looked at the scrolls hanging in the *tokonoma* (alcove) and others that Terayama-sensei brought out and hung around the walls of the room. These were candidate objects for the exhibition of Zen calligraphy and painting from his collection that was subsequently held at the Victoria and Albert Museum in the autumn of 2001.

Business over, so to speak, we proceeded to the kitchen to partake of an excellent dinner – the first of many I was to enjoy at Terayama-sensei's house – prepared by Yō-san. It was during this meal that I learnt of Terayama-sensei's love of food, our common interest in ceramics, and of his penchant for good *sake*. I remember giggling to myself and thinking, 'aha, it is only a true man of Zen who can show his guests hospitality with the same intensity as he engages in the ascetic rigours of his discipline.'

Intensity, to a degree that took me quite a time to become comfortable with, was very much an aspect of Terayama-sensei's disposition and demeanour. It revealed itself with explosive force in the demonstration of *kendō* he gave during the series of events accompanying the opening of the V&A's 2001 Zen calligraphy and painting exhibition. There was no question about how he could cut through and see straight into the heart of things. And he would not mince his words or refrain from speaking his mind. And yet, or rather one should say in addition, Terayama-sensei was an exceptionally kind and caring person. Without this dimension to his charisma, he would not have gathered around him the large and devoted group of followers who have been so devastated by his untimely death. The beautiful piece of calligraphy (page 71) he so kindly bequeathed to the Victoria and Albert Museum remains as testament to his generosity, and to his mastery of the art he loved so much.

Rupert Faulkner

Senior Curator, Japan, Asian Department,
Victoria and Albert Museum

INTRODUCTION: PART 1

By Sarah Moate

This elegant image of a bamboo sword, *kendō* helmet with flowing cords and inscription in two columns of cursive script, written towards the end of his life in 1888, reveals the life and concerns of Yamaoka Tesshū. The exhibition at the Victoria and Albert museum that this book was originally conceived to accompany, marks the 120th anniversary of Tesshū's passing away.

The calligraphy is exquisitely executed in subtle tonal gradations that have arisen naturally as the brush touched the paper and the lines appear perforated by the rhythm of the calligrapher's breath. In the Song period (960-1279), the distinguished Chinese scholar-painter Su T'ung-po (Su Shih, 1036-1101), remarked that "Before you can paint bamboo, it must first grow in your inmost heart." This image by Tesshū, who was a master swordsman as well as a practitioner of Zen and calligraphy, is clearly based on lived experience. The inscription reads,

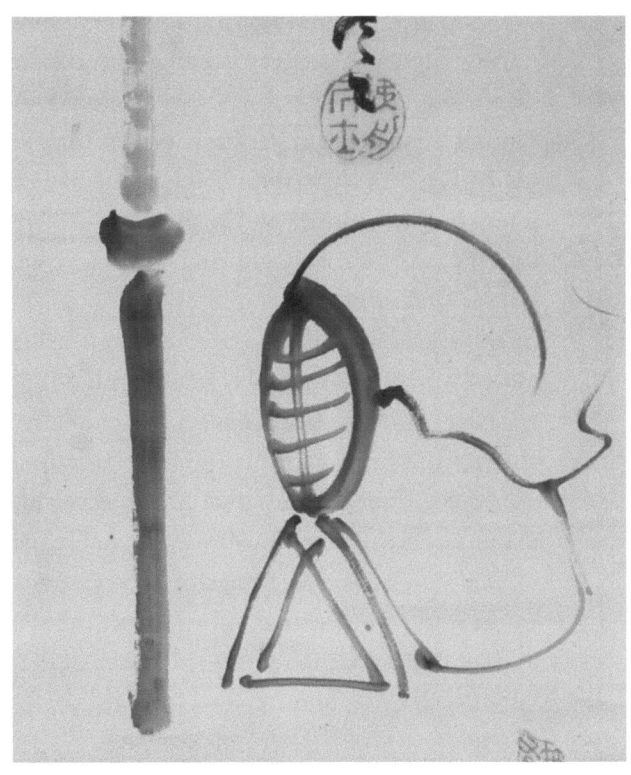

　剣術の極意は風の柳かな
　　　正四位山岡鐵太郎書
"The mystique of fencing is like willows in the wind.
Yamaoka Tetsutarō – Honoured with the Senior Fourth Court Rank."

This alludes to an image drawn from nature. The branches of a willow tree are pliant yet resilient, becoming one with the natural forces of the wind rather than resisting it. The image conjured up of the willow branches yielding and moving freely in tandem with the invisible wind is poetic. It can also be seen as a metaphor for the ideal state of mind, flexible, free of attachment and transcending the usual limitations of self.

Calligraphy in this context is regarded as a 'picture of the mind' and its origins lie in China. In Zen terms it reveals the depth of the Zen calligrapher's state of being, as discernible in the physical traces of *sumi* ink brushed on paper in the immediacy of the moment, which are directly and spontaneously painted with no re-touching. The transmission of this state of mind can be perceived in the calligraphy years after being

written.

It is interesting to note that the monthly Zen calligraphy and painting appreciation sessions at Professor Terayama Tanchū's residence entailed reflection on the calligraphies in silence, and a short period of *zazen* preceded the main lecture and exchange. Usually five scrolls would be displayed in the *tokonoma* (alcove) and elements such as theme, scale, materials, compositional balance and spacing would be considered, as well as terms not so familiar to Western viewers such as *ki-in seidō* (気韻生動), which literally means 'alive and resonating with vital energy', and *bokki* (墨気) the 'vitality' of the *sumi* ink.[1] *Ki-in seidō* is one of the six principles of painting laid down in *The Classified Records of Painters of Former Times*, by Hsieh Ho, (479-?).

Su T'ung-po commented,

"Mountain, rock, bamboo, tree, ripples in water, mist and cloud – none of these has a fixed form. But, nonetheless, they all have a constant inner line. This is what must guide the mind of the painter."

This inner line is the essence of the calligraphic tradition which Yamaoka Tesshū aspired to. It can be said that the three spare lines which form the bamboo sword on the left of the composition, suggest not just the presence and absence of the form of the sword itself, but the presence of the practitioner and ultimately a 'Way' of being.

Zen (S: *dhyana*; C: *Ch'an*), arrived in Japan in the late twelfth century, via India and China. Sōtō Zen with its emphasis on *zazen* and Rinzai Zen with its focus on *satori* and *kōan* practice, both taught the importance of awakening to one's true inner self and letting go of the ego-self. During the Edo period (1600-1868), under Tokugawa rule, Neo-Confucianism became predominant, especially influencing the samurai officials of the period. In the mid-17th century, Chinese monks arrived in Japan and formed a third school, Ōbaku Zen, which had a profound cultural effect as the monks brought with them many aspects of Ming dynasty culture, including brushwork. And even after Japan re-opened to the West in 1853, Zen cultural ideals of serenity, elegance and self-cultivation continue to have a deep effect from those first origins. In the 21st century the refinement and precision of the tea-ceremony, Zen calligraphy or the martial arts such as *kendō* or *kyudō* (Japanese archery), are a meditative experience in themselves and have a universal spirit.

Tesshū is renowned for his statement that swordsmanship, Zen and calligraphy are identical in their aspiration to the state of no-mind. Known in Japanese as *mu-shin*, it is a state beyond thoughts, emotions and expectations. It is known that in the first years of the Meiji era (1868-1912), Yamaoka Tesshū owned a rare manuscript copy of *Shōnan kattō-roku*, (record of Kamakura *kōan*) recording Zen paradoxical riddles given to warriors by the first immigrant Zen teachers from China.[2]

The essence of Kamakura Zen was to attain a state of mind free from mental and emotional attachments, to let go of the ego-self. These *kōan* were often made spontaneously and revolved around items of everyday life, such as a tea-cup or a mirror, to bring the warrior students to the essential first realisation. Case 44 in the *Shōnan kattō-roku* is entitled 'Wielding the Spear With Hands Empty', which essentially is about investigating where attention resides when using a spear. Although Japanese sword form requires the practitioner to commit both hands to the sword, true understanding of the form does not lie solely in the hands. *Tanden* (C: *tantien*), the central abdominal area of the body, is thought to be where true consciousness arises. In Chinese texts on brushwork there are also detailed technical instructions on the relationship between *tanden*, the way of holding the brush and the notion of emptiness. To reach this state of no-mind one of the key elements is repetition, whether it is continually repeating a sword *kata* (prescribed sequence of movements), chanting a *sutra* or brushing the same characters again and again. Although the brush is held in one hand the wrist is not the focus of attention, the whole body and mind is engaged.

In *Zen and Japanese Culture*, Daisetz Suzuki (1870-1966), devoted a section to Yamaoka Tesshū, focusing on his Zen method whereby his students trained to physical and mental exhaustion after which a stimulus was given that unexpectedly tapped a source of previously hidden energy. Suzuki comments that Tesshū knew from his long experience in Zen that "A man has to die, and leave his ordinary consciousness in order to awaken the unconscious."[3] Tesshū was so dedicated to his study of Zen that he founded the Zenshōan Temple in Yanaka and the Tesshūji Temple in Suruga (modern Shizuoka City). Tesshū's grave is located at Zenshōan, and even today many people gather in his honour for an annual memorial ceremony on July 19.

Under the tutelage of Iwasa Ittei (d. 1858), the 51st head of the Jubokudō school of calligraphy, Tesshū mastered the writing styles of the Chinese master Wang Xizhi (J: Ō Gishi, 303-361) and Kōbō Daishi (774-835, also known as Kūkai), whose calligraphy he revered, eventually becoming the 52nd head of the Jubokudō school.[4]

The extant calligraphies by Tesshū include a variety of formats, such as hanging and hand scrolls, fans, screens, albums, poem cards and wooden sign-boards, he is also

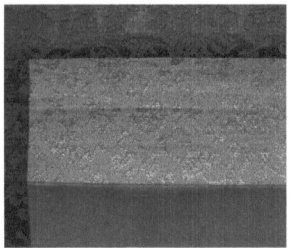

Detail of *ichimonji* (immediate surround at top and bottom of the calligraphy) of "Shrine of the Deity", 1885. Stylised flower pattern on silk brocade.

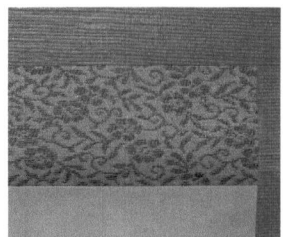

Detail of *ichimonji* of *kendō* helmet and bamboo sword, 1886. Stylised flower pattern on silk brocade.

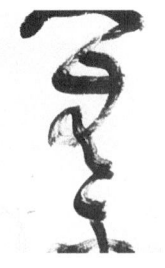
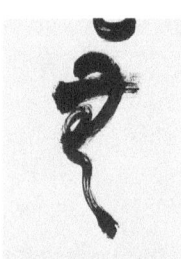

The character *mu* (無)

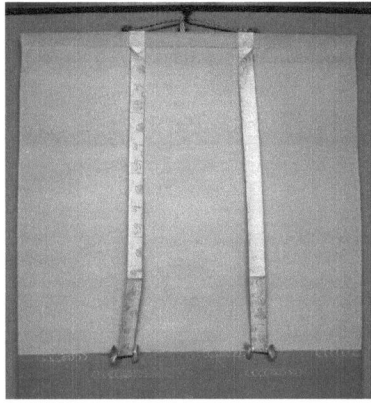

Detail of *ichimonji* and *futai* (hanging decorative strips) of "Three Pines", 1888. This is a formal style of mounting. The brocades chosen for the immediate surrounding area and strips of silk hanging from the rod at the top of the scroll have been chosen carefully to subtly complement the calligraphy. The stylised decoration is a cloud motif, often used in Buddhist art to symbolise the transience of life.

known to have written calligraphy on *fusuma* (sliding doors). Even today, in the centre of Ginza in Tokyo, an illuminated sign over the door of 'Kimura-ya' (a popular bakery dating from 1869) bears a reproduction of Tesshū's original inscription for the founder's sign board.

Calligraphy has its origins in China with the earliest pictographs being carved into shell and bone around 3,500 years ago. Tesshū's thorough education in both copying and contemplating classic texts of Chinese calligraphy as well as that of Zen masters permeated his thought. Tesshū's brushwork of the 'Sutra of the Bequeathed Teaching', (J: *Butsu yui kyō-gyō*; C: *I-chiao-ching*) is from the Zenshōan collection (p. 93). This *sutra* is thought to be the last sermon of the Buddha, and emphasises the importance of the precepts, meditation and wisdom. It is chanted in Japanese temples on

February 15, during *Nedane*, a memorial service held for the Buddha who is believed to have passed away on this day, although the *sutra* itself can be written out at any time.

Written formally in *kaisho* or regular script in vertical columns, it reads from top-right to bottom-left. Buddhist sutras were translated from Sanskrit to Chinese characters and are usually written in regular script which is easily read. Each character is written independently and in a block form. The regular script is similar in structure to scribe's script (*reisho*), with clearly delineated horizontal and vertical strokes, giving an overall effect which is formal and classic in feel. *Sutra* writing is carried out as an act of devotion, and Tesshū's brushed characters which would have been executed in one sitting with no retouching, are flawlessly formed. The character *mu* (無), appears three times in the sections of the *sutra* illustrated. Reading from right to left it occurs on sheet one, column five, character seven, again on sheet two, column five, character one and on sheet three, column six, character 13, each time written freshly, in the immediacy of the moment. The regular script form is written with 12 strokes, starting with the top left-hand diagonal stroke and ending with the four dots at the bottom of the character. The line itself appears to penetrate the paper that it is written on, suffused with *ki*. This work is considered outstanding in Yamaoka Tesshū's oeuvre and is testimony to the refined excellence of his regular script.

Perhaps the most surprising of the images by Tesshū illustrated on these pages is that of the *yuki-daruma* or snowman. The main form of the snowman has been brushed in one fluid stroke, and the mouth is depicted as down-turned, as if in serious concentration. The inscription has also been brushed with economic means, in cursive script, ranging from the initial rich tone of wet brush marks to the dry brush strokes at the end.

廓然無聖是什麼　鉄舟高歩
"Vast emptiness – nothing sacred!
Tesshū kōho"

It refers to the episode when the Emperor of China asked Bodhidharma, the Great Patriarch of Zen, 'What is the first principle of Buddhism?' Bodhidharma replied, 'Vast emptiness, nothing sacred!' It is taken from the *Blue Cliff Record*, a *kōan* collection compiled in the eleventh century by Xue Tou. Bodhidharma—or Daruma in Japanese—is represented here as a 'snowman'. A snowman is made of ice which readily changes form and becomes water. The snowman's lack of a stable shape can be likened to the formlessness of the Buddha nature. Tesshū may well have also had in mind the opening line of Hakuin Zenji's *Song of Zazen*. "All sentient beings are essentially Buddhas. As with water and ice, there is no ice apart from water, apart from sentient beings, there are no Buddhas."[5] The plate on page 85 shows a Bodhidharma from the Zenshōan collection. Drawn in profile, this Daruma has also been brushed deftly, in a few strokes. In this case the abbreviated inscription in cursive script, reads from left to right. As is the custom with images of Bodhidharma, the head is placed facing to the left of the composition. Tesshū's signature and seal impression are placed to the right, to the rear of Bodhidharma's head. This expresses humility on the part of the Zen artist. Both inscriptions contain the cursive script form of the character *mu*, which is written here in two strokes, commencing with the horizontal stroke. In the image of the *yuki-daruma*, it is contained in the first column on the right, third character down, about midway in the unbroken column of flowing script. In the painting of Bodhidharma it is the last character in the far left-hand column, written separately from the first two characters and appears to float unattached, in space.

Although Zen calligraphy is written in seconds, it is cultivated over a lifetime of moments. Even if one cannot read the characters, the traces of ink on the paper reveal Tesshū's heart and mind.

Figures A-D show Tesshū's signature from ages 37-52. It is possible to discern the transformation in his calligraphy.

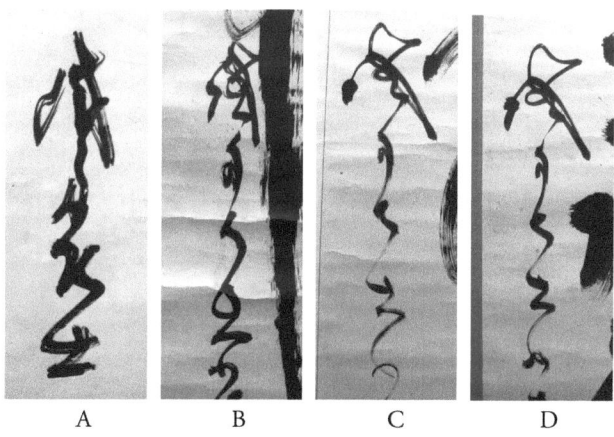

A   B   C   D

A. Age 37. (See "*Masa ni eifū o urayamu*" p. 27.)
B. Age 45, after his enlightenment experience of March 30, 1880. (See "*Ryū Ko*" p. 33.)
C. Age 50. (See "*Jinen no fūgetsu jō tsukiru koto nashi*" p. 39.)
D. Age 52. (See "*Kinshin shishu shin ai esu*" p. 31.)

1. Ōmori Sōgen Rōshi (1904-1994), of the Tenryūji Temple lineage has this to say about *bokki*: "The clarity of the *bokki*, the *ki* in the ink, indicates the level of insight. *Bokki* is not only seen with the eyes, it is sensed with the *hara*, the physical and spiritual centre of one's body. *Bokki* reveals the calligrapher's inner light. *Bokki* is not identical to the brushstroke, but it is not independent either – it cannot be dissected or arranged into neat compartments." Ōmori Sōgen and Terayama Katsujō, John Stevens (trans.), *Zen and the Art of Calligraphy – The Essence of Sho*, Routledge and Kegan Paul, 1983, p.10

2. Imai Fukuzan noted in his publication about this text (1925) that Tesshū was given a manuscript copy of *Shōnan kattō-roku* (by the Zen priest Shōjō of Ryūtakuji Temple in Izu. See *Samurai Zen – The Warrior Koans*, Trevor Leggett, Routledge, 2003. p.31

3. D.T. Suzuki, *Zen and Japanese Culture*, Rutland, Vermont: Tuttle, 1959, p.196.

4. 'Jubokudō' literally means 'the Way of going into wood'. It refers to an episode concerning Wang Xizhi in Zhang Huai Guan's (active 714-760) *Classifications of Calligraphy*, according to which the Chinese characters that Wang had written on a wooden signboard were found to have seeped three inches deep into the wood by the carver who engraved the board. In Japan the term appears in treatises on calligraphy from the late Heian period (794-1185) until the Edo period (1600-1868).

5. Hakuin Ekaku (1686-1769), is considered the most influential Zen monk of the past 500 years. He made the Shōinji Temple in Hara (modern Shizuoka Prefecture), the centre for the revitalisation of the Rinzai Zen tradition. He often wrote calligraphy with one character larger in scale, emphasising his message. His calligraphy was greatly admired by Tesshū.

INTRODUCTION: PART 2

By Alex Bennett

The sword in Japan has occupied a position of reverence in mythology and warrior tales throughout the centuries. Thomas McClatchie, a British envoy to Japan during the Meiji period (1868-1912) and a great aficionado of Japan's sword culture commented on its importance to the Japanese.

> "There is no country in the world where the sword has received so much honour and renown as in Japan. Regarded as of divine origin, dear to the general as a symbol of authority, cherished by the samurai as a part of himself, considered by the common people as their protection against violence, how can we wonder to find it called the living soul of the samurai?"

Indeed, the Japanese *katana* is renowned throughout the world for its beauty and devastating cutting power. They are adored as superb examples of artistic craftsmanship while simultaneously feared as lethal weapons. As the "living soul" of the samurai, the *katana* held spiritual significance that exceeded any other weapon or implement.

A warrior's profession is war. The primary objective for the samurai in battle was to take the life of his enemy, or die in trying. The samurai accepted, embraced in fact, the inevitability of his mortality; and ironically, preparedness for death in combat was a crucial factor in his survival. The famous medieval daimyo Uesugi Kenshin once said, "Those who cling to life die; and those who defy death live." Samurai trained in swordsmanship to cultivate technical skill, and also to strengthen their mind and remove any chinks in their spiritual armour.

As the *katana* was used with two hands, the samurai was unable to wield a shield for protection. Each time his sword was drawn, the encounter was a fight to the death, and the only line of defence was to attack without holding back, with no concern for the consequences.

The various martial schools (*ryūha*) that arose from the 15th century trained the warrior to subdue his fears. The schools taught a superlative combination of body, mind and technique which made the warrior invincible in battle—both technically and spiritually—through a supposed transcendence of concerns for life and death.

The reality of death, and how to manage fear was also contemplated through the study of Zen. For example, in the house-code of the Takeda clan, warriors were advised to, "Be devoted to the study of Zen. Zen has no secrets other than seriously thinking about birth and death." Although Buddhism is generally pacifistic, meditating on the "transience of all things" assisted warriors in coping with the trauma of taking, or forfeiting life. Hence, Zen was readily adopted into warrior culture as an integral part of their edification.

At first, Zen was a "spiritual supplement" of sorts to the samurai. As martial *ryūha* became more sophisticated in terms of technical and philosophical teachings during the peaceful early-modern period, the goal of swordsmanship transformed, and the target became the enemy within, or the purging of one's own evil desires.

By the time Japan was pacified in the Tokugawa period (1603-1868), opportunities for warriors to demonstrate their prowess in battle became virtually nonexistent, but they were still expected to continue training in the military arts, even if the practical necessity was no longer apparent. To use the oft quoted cliché in martial arts research, training evolved from *bujutsu* (martial techniques for killing) to *bugei* (martial art), and then later into *budō* (martial Way) where the goal was to "give life" rather than take it. The martial traditions from this period gradually enveloped a "spirit of non-lethality" akin to Zen.

Through the process of learning martial techniques, the warrior sought to acquire a higher spiritual state of mind, and training became a

"Way" of self-development. The question of death still remained a central component in the samurai ethos, albeit a somewhat idealised notion. The "ideal of death" was enacted through unrelenting training in the martial arts where an acceptance or preparedness for death was in effect nullifying the self in the ongoing pursuit of *satori* or enlightenment.

Samurai were obligated to maintain military readiness as "keepers of the peace", and cultivate their humanity to be beacons of moral perfection. Swordsmanship became a vehicle to achieve this, and thus transformed into a path to enlightenment, just like Zen. The sword changed from a weapon of destruction into a tool for spiritual emancipation through ascetic training.

The correlation between swordsmanship and Zen, and questions of death and enlightenment are not difficult to envisage in samurai culture, but what of calligraphy? This may be one of the most difficult connections for the uninitiated to make.

Thomas Jefferson sent a letter to Thomas Paine in 1796 in which he wrote, "Go on doing with your pen what in other times was done with the sword." The inference is that the pen is mightier than the sword; an adage that has much weight in Western civilisation. But the pen (brush) in Japan is considered the equivalent of the sword for reasons other than its potential to influence people for good or bad. Both the sword and the brush were "internalised" as vehicles to travel the path to enlightenment. A well-known Japanese maxim states, "There are many paths up the mountain, but all view the same moon from the summit." Swordsmanship, Zen, and brushwork were equivalent in this sense, and one was not necessarily superior to the other, as long as the adept surrendered himself unconditionally to his ascetic quest.

Zen has always had a natural affinity with the art of calligraphy, and many coveted works still in existence were brushed by Zen masters and warriors. Like the warrior who faces his enemy with a razor-sharp blade, liberated from any concern for the outcome of the encounter, the Zen painter approaches his waxen paper with a blank mind and no concern for beauty.

Ultimately, the calligrapher, the warrior and the monk share the intention of nullifying the ego in order to come closer to understanding the truth of being. It is not indifference to life, but an acceptance of life and death as a set, and the self as being at one with the cosmos, and vice versa. One who was successful in grasping this concept was considered to be enlightened. The sublime beauty of the calligraphy that the enlightened master produced, or flawless technique in any other activity he engaged in, was not the goal *per se,* but merely a consequence of his awakening.

The works featured in this book were brushed by a samurai warrior and true master of *ken-zen-sho.* Yamaoka Tesshū served as a retainer to the Tokugawa shogunate, and was a pivotal figure in the Meiji Restoration of 1868. In 1862, he and Takahashi Deishū (1835-1903), whose work also appears in this book, formed a crack unit of skilled swordsmen to monitor anti-shogunate activities. When the imperial forces entered Edo in 1868 under the command of Saigō Takamori, the acting commandant of the shogunal forces, Katsu Kaishū relied on Tesshū to steer initial negotiations to try and avoid open conflict. Tesshū's skills in diplomacy were attributed to having staved a bloody confrontation, and enabled the peaceful surrender of Edo castle to the new imperial government. After the restoration, Tesshū served as a trusted aide to Emperor Meiji, a rare privilege for former Tokugawa retainers.

The life of Tesshū is shrouded in mystery, and it is often difficult to discern fact from fiction. Tesshū was a physically large man for his era, and had an equally domineering spirit. In the martial arts training hall, he had the reputation of a 'demon', and was considered to be somewhat eccentric and nonconformist.

After years of searching for a worthy opponent, Tesshū met his match with Asari Matashichirō Yoshiaki. Upon hearing of Asari's fearsome reputation, Tesshū went to his *dōjō* and challenged him to a bout. According to reports of the encounter, the contest lasted for many hours with no decisive result. Tesshū tried using his superior size and strength to defeat Asari, but his attacks were rendered ineffective. Finally, Tesshū knocked Asari onto the *dōjō* floor when the two clashed in a flurry of techniques. Asari took off his fencing mask and declared the match to be over. Tesshū was greatly satisfied with his victory, and smugly said that Asari was indeed a skilled opponent, but not skilled enough.

Asari retorted that he was in fact the victor, and explained to the disbelieving Tesshū that as he was falling to the ground, he delivered a decisive cut to the right side of Tesshū's torso. If they were using live blades instead of bamboo staves, Asari declared, Tesshū would have been "cleft in twain". Tesshū removed his protector and saw to his astonishment that the slats had indeed been split. According to tradition, Tesshū admitted defeat and immediately became Asari's disciple.

Only after 17 years of fanatical training under Asari's tutorship and studying Zen did the overwhelming specter of Asari in his mind suddenly disappear. He is said to have experienced a kind of spiritual liberation when he was 45 years old, and this epiphany signified a turning point in his swordsmanship, Zen, and calligraphy.

Tesshū inspired his students to discover for themselves the "sword of no-sword" by losing the self in training. To facilitate an understanding of this concept, Tesshū devised the gruelling test known as *tachikiri-geiko*, where the candidate participated in hundreds of continuous bouts over a number of days. In Daisetz T. Suzuki's classic book *Zen and Japanese Culture* (Tuttle, 1959), there is a fascinating eye-witness account of this harsh training. The candidate was Kagawa Zenjirō.

"On the third day of these strenuous exercises, I could hardly raise myself from bed, and had to ask my wife's help. When she tried to lift me she felt as if raising a lifeless corpse and unconsciously withdrew her hands which she had placed underneath my back. And then I felt her tears on my face. Hardening myself to the utmost, I admonished her not to be so weak-hearted. Somehow I succeeded with her help in raising the upper part of my body.

I had to use a cane to walk up to the training hall. I had also to be helped to put on my protecting equipment. As I took my position, the contestants began to crowd in. After a while I noticed one member come in and approach the master (Tesshū) to ask his permission to take part in the exercises. The master permitted him right away. I looked at him and at once realized that he was the one noted for his rascality, who, disregarding the swordsman's usage, would thrust his bamboo sword to the naked throat behind the protecting gorget and keep it up even after he was already struck over his head by his victorious opponent.

When I saw him coming up to me, I made up my mind that this would be my last combat, for I might not survive the contest. With this determination I felt within myself the surging up of a new energy. I was quite a different person. My sword returned to its proper position. I approached him now fully conscious of my fresh inner surge and lifting up the sword over my head, was ready to strike him with one blow of it. At this moment, came the master's emphatic command to stop, and I dropped my sword."
(p. 196)

Tesshū knew that at this instant that his student had been liberated from the shackles of his ego, and had come to realise the "sword of no-sword".
Although we can only imagine the fierceness of Tesshū's swordsmanship, he bequeathed us a legacy

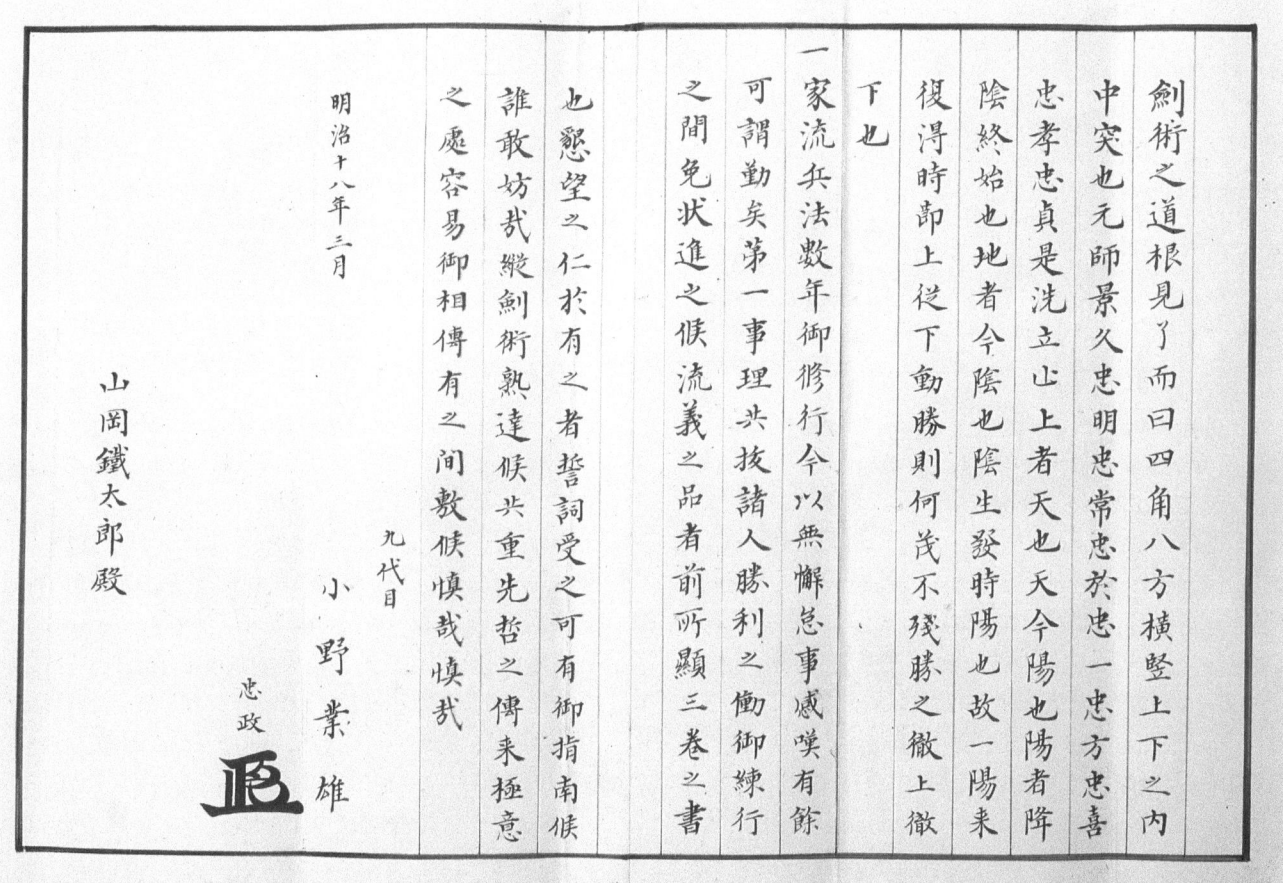

This document is the Ittō-ryū licence of mastery presented to Yamaoka Tesshū in March 1885 by the school's ninth Sōke, Ono Norio. *Sumi* ink on paper. Zenshōan collection.

of magnificent specimens of calligraphy which we can still marvel at today. Fortunately, he also left us documents explaining the path he travelled to enlightenment in *ken-zen-sho*. According to Professor Terayama's research, by comparing his calligraphy before and after the age of 45 when he became enlightened, one can clearly see *ki-in seidō* in the characters, brushed by a man who knew *mu-shin* (no-mind) and could act free of any mental or emotional attachments.

It is difficult even for a novice to deny that there is something special about his works. Even though they are well over a century old, the *sumi* ink seems to shine as if it was still wet. One can feel the life force in each brush stroke, and the warmth and compassion of the man who wrote them.

Professor Terayama Tanchū was so intrigued by

the life of Tesshū and his works, that he collected and studied them for much of his career. Through his achievements in *ken-zen-sho*, both as a scholar and a veritable master of all three "Ways", he has bequeathed us valuable knowledge to help us comprehend the somewhat nebulous world of these paths to enlightenment, and how they are relevant to people in the 21st century. Although genuine understanding is impossible without actual engagement and many years of rigorous hands-on study, Professor Terayama has kept the flow of wisdom intact between the generations, and has made it accessible for people of all cultures.

As he mentions at the end of his essay, all of these works represent a high point of Japanese culture, but are also an asset for all of humanity.

KEN-ZEN-SHO   The Relevance of Swordsmanship, Zen and Calligraphy

By Terayama Tanchū

'Ken'

Japanese swordsmanship is commonly referred to as *kenjutsu*, and its history is as ancient as the craft of making swords in Japan. Leaving aside historical details, swordsmanship matured into a way for training the mind to overcome fears of death and dealing with life's anxieties.

During the medieval period, extending from the Gempei wars of the twelfth century through to the Ashikaga shogunate of the 14th and 15th centuries, Japan was constantly in a state of civil strife. Warriors studied the science of war in the search of ubiquitous principles to enhance their martial prowess. They developed pedagogical systems to learn the arts of war based on these laws. This gave rise to specific schools (*ryūha*) of *kenjutsu* where the typical syllabus provided a technical and spiritual framework to contain their fears, and accept the 'inevitability of death' (*shōji ketsujō*).

Representative of such schools were the Kage-ryū of western Japan, and the Tenshinshō-den Katori Shintō-ryū in the east, both evolving in the 15th century. Of particular interest are claims that the progenitors of these traditions were bequeathed divine wisdom from supernatural beings after completing harsh regimes of austere training and prayer.

With the progression of time and continued technical development, ideals on perfecting the mind became central to the course of study. Philosophical concepts were conceived by great swordsmen such as Kamiizumi Ise no Kami's '*fumetsu-no-kokoro*' (eternal mind); Miyamoto Musashi's '*iwao-no-mi*' (the body of a rock); Harigaya Sekiun's '*muju-shin*' (non-abiding mind); Tsuji Gettan's '*ippō-mugai*' (one true way); Kamiya Denshinsai's '*jikishin*' (upright heart); Yamaoka Tesshū's '*semui*' (giver of fearlessness). These are all teachings denoting a transcendental state of mind underscoring the inevitability of death, and preparedness to face it. In this sense, *kenjutsu* progressed from being combat systems with techniques for the sole purpose of killing in order to stay alive, into deep philosophical "Ways" (*michi*) of training in the techniques as a vehicle for enlightenment.

'Zen'

During the Kamakura period (1185-1333), Hōjō Tokimune (1251-84), the eighth shogunal regent, lived in a perilous age constantly faced with the threat of violence. He learned from the Zen monk Wu-hsueh (J: Mugaku) that the greatest utility of Zen was to bring to light both the meaning of life and death to overcome such anxieties. Dōgen (1200-1253), founder of the Sōtō sect of Zen Buddhism in 1227, reiterated this principle in the *Shōbō genzō* (*Treasury of the Eye of the True Dharma*). "The most important task for monks is to elucidate the meaning of life and death."

Shūhō Myōchō (1282-1337), also known as Daitō Kokushi, was a monk of the Rinzai sect of Zen Buddhism. He taught that the most important point of Zen is "self explanation" (*koji kyūmei*). In his work *Yuikai* (*The Admonition*) he explained that the sole objective was to discover the "true self" and live accordingly. The true self cannot be simply quantified in terms of years, weight or height, but is an inestimable entity without solid form. That is why Dōgen declared in *Shōbō genzō*, the 'self' that pervades the ten-directional world, or fills the whole earth, is one's true body.

Human beings have long been conscious of their mortality and feebleness in the greater scheme of the universe. The long path to surpass all mortal limitations and access a supreme realm resulted in these revelations. To this purpose, people engage in the study of Zen to "know the self". "To learn one's self is to forget one's self." (*Shōbō genzō – Genjō kōan*). By forgetting the self, and eliminating the self, only then will the real self be revealed. "Just let go of one's body and mind, casting them into the house of Buddha." (*Shōbō genzō – Shōji*).

In this way, the student of Zen is able to nullify the self mainly through practising *zazen*, and eventually be awoken to the 'primary life'. Zen, it could be said, matured as a means of independently living one's primary life.

'Sho'

The pulse of this 'primary life' was also a factor in the appraisal of first-rate brushwork in the *Ku Hua P'in Lu* (J: *Kogahin-roku – The Classified Records of Painters of Former Times*) by Hsieh Ho (J: Sha Kaku) (479-?). Although the title indicates paintings, the Chinese considered painting and brushwork to be in the same genre, so it also applied to calligraphy.

However, even before that, Wang Xizhi (J: Ō Gishi 303-361) was a famous Chinese calligrapher widely referred to as the 'Sage of Painting'. In a collection of his letters (*Jironsho*) he states, "The maturity (*seijuku*) of the painter Zhang Chih (J: Chōshi) far exceeds mine. His whole heart permeates each brushstroke (*seisaku*)…" The word *seijuku* refers to the technical skill of the calligrapher, and *seisaku* to the spiritual qualities of applying the brush with all of one's heart. In other words, ancient paintings and calligraphy works were valued depending on technical and spiritual quality, and outstanding ability in both facets was the highest aspiration.

Kūkai (also known as Kōbō Daishi 774-835) was a famous Buddhist priest of the early Heian period. He considered calligraphy and art to be the product of "dissipating all that is contained in the heart" (*Shōryō-shū*). Huang Shangu (J: Kōsankoku 1045-1105), counted as one of the finest calligraphers and poets of the Northern Song dynasty, recorded that the works he brushed when he was in his forties "did not contain his brush." He explained that calligraphy that 'contained the brush' was synonymous to a Zen poem's crucial pivotal character or word (*shigan*) that made it complete. In other words without the 'brush', he considered his work incomplete and lacking the 'life breath force' (*ki-in seidō*) needed to give the work beauty.

The *Jubokushō* (1352) is an explanation of examples of *shodō* (calligraphy) brushed by Son'en Shinnō (1298-1356) for Emperor Gokōgon (1338-1374). He writes, "A superior work of calligraphy is like a living entity, just as if it contains spirit and soul…Its spirit is ubiquitous and it has no flaws whatsoever…To state the consequence of this 'Way', enlightenment in Buddhist law is discernable in the perfection of worldly arts."

Therefore, calligraphy (*sho*) was perceived as being far more profound than just writing visually pleasing characters. For this, the most important ingredient was spirited utilisation of one's 'primary life'.

Training in swordsmanship (*ken*) and Zen were considered ways of learning how to transcend concerns of life and death. Training required an attitude of 'self-annihilation' to return to the transcendental state of one's 'primary life'. Works of calligraphy were, and still are, valued highly when the artist demonstrates the ability to tap into the same life pulse.

Two Masters of *Ken-zen-sho-* Musashi and Tesshū

There are a number of notable individuals throughout Japanese history who travelled the path of *ken-zen-sho*. Great warriors such as Yagyū Munenori (1571-1645) immediately spring to mind, but I will limit my analysis to Miyamoto Musashi (1582-1645) and Yamaoka Tesshū (1836-1888).

Miyamoto Musashi was born into the Tahara family of Harima-no-kuni (modern-day Hyōgo Prefecture), and became the adopted son and student of Munisai, a master of the *jitte* (metal truncheon). Given his lineage, Musashi was destined to walk the path of the warrior since birth. His first encounter in mortal combat was at age 13 against Arima Kihei, a swordsman of the Shintō-ryū tradition. It is recorded in his celebrated military treatise *Gorin no sho* that by the time he was 28 or 29, he had fought in over 60 duels without being defeated.

However, after the age of 30, he surmised that he had never beaten his opponents in accordance with the true principles of the sword. Instead, his successes had been a product of luck or the ineptitude of his opponents, rather than a genuine understanding of high strategy (*hyōhō* or *heihō*).

It also states in the initial pages of *Gorin no sho*,

> "I relentlessly trained my body and mind and only gained and understanding of strategy around the age of 50. Since that day, I have lived without need of searching further into the Way. When I apply the principles of strategy to the various artistic Ways, I am no longer in need of a tutor for any of them."

It took him 20 years of struggle and great hardship to reach this level where he learned to completely 'nullify' the self. Everything he had searched for became apparent, and was infused in every aspect of his world. It was a complete about turn. The principles of strategy which now emanated from Musashi's being could be applied to all other artistic pursuits such as calligraphy, carving and metalwork which he was able to master independently. Engrossed with these arts from childhood, he had polished his technique for 20 years. Enlightenment to the universal principles of all arts brought life to his work once he realised that total mastery of one 'Way' was in essence the same as every 'Way'.

These principles are perfectly germane to the laws of Zen. The influence Zen had on Musashi is evident in his repetitive use of Zen terms such as *jikishin* (true mind) and *ginmi* (to know the truth through exploring and experience). He also painted many quintessential Zen works of Daruma and Hotei. The chapter in *Gorin no sho* entitled *Kū* (the void) is particularly relevant to Zen.

Many treatises on military strategy arranged content in accordance with the five elements of earth, water, fire, wind, and the void. *Gorin no sho*, often translated into English as *The Book of Five Rings*, was influenced by the Zen teaching of *Go-i*

or "The Five Ranks" of enlightenment. These were discovered by the Chinese Zen master and founder of the Sōtō sect, Tung-shan Liang-chieh (J: Tōzan Ryōkai), and Ts'ao-shan Pen-chi (J: Sōzan Honjaku). There are many variations and interpretations, but I refer here to what is called *Shō-hen Go-i*: *Shō-chū-hen* (The Apparent within the Real); *Hen-chū-shō* (The Real within the Apparent); *Shō-chū-rai* (The Coming from within the Real); *Ken-chū-shi* (The Arrival at Mutual Integration); *Ken-chū-tō* (Unity Attained).

The final stage of *Ken-chū-tō* is where form and emptiness fully interpenetrate. At this level, actions are instantaneous and unconscious. In the "Ten Ox-herding Pictures"—representations of the ten stages of the Zen Way to enlightenment shown through ten pictures of an ox and its herder—this equates with the juncture of "To Return to the Origin" to "Entering the City with Bliss-bestowing Hands". The "Void" chapter in Musashi's *Gorin no sho* is closest to this notion of enlightenment.

In the introduction of *Gorin no sho*, Musashi states, "In composing this treatise, I do not borrow from the ancient Buddhist or Confucian writings." I believe that he had already fully digested the ancient wisdom and simplified the concepts in his writing.

A more recent master of *ken-zen-sho* and the focus of this book was Yamaoka Tesshū (Tetsutarō) (1836-88). He commenced studies of calligraphy when he was seven or eight years of age under his mother Iso. One of the words he was initially taught to write was *chū-kō* (忠孝). He asked his mother what it meant. She replied that *chū* referred to maintaining a correct and loyal mind when serving one's lord, and *kō* means piety to this way. The young Tetsutarō then asked "Do you uphold such bearing?" His mother remained silent for a while, and then shedding a tear she said, "Oh Tetsu, I always try to hold such an attitude in my heart. But alas, I am a worthless woman and waver in my commitment. I implore you to become a man who lives up to these ideals."

When he was 13, his father Takatomi beseeched him, "A man who follows the martial path must never forget where his obligations of loyalty lie." This entailed, he continued, "First and foremost learning correct form through the martial arts, and training the mind in the principles of Zen." When he was 29 Tesshū wrote, "This is what motivated me to study these two ways." It provided the basis for his future development, and history clearly demonstrates that he upheld the virtue of loyalty.

He wrote of his studies of *ken-zen-sho* in his youth and I would like to quote him directly. Firstly, in regards to swordsmanship:

"When I was a young boy I studied swordsmanship, and learned the laws of Zen. Whatever I felt in my mind I tried to put into form, and have continued my study to this day. When I was nine years old, I entered the tutelage of Kusumi Kantekisai and learned swordsmanship. I then studied under Inoue Kiyotora, Chiba Shūsaku, Saitō, and Momoi. I broadened my training by engaging in countless matches with swordsmen representing many different schools. For more than 20 years I trained relentlessly without reaching an understanding of the deeper principles that I sought. I searched in vain for a truly enlightened master of swordsmanship to aid me in my quest. Finally, I met Asari Matashichirō Yoshiaki, a master of the Ittō-ryū tradition. He was the second son of Nakanishi Tanemasa of the Okudaira family, and the successor of the school created by Itō Ittōsai Kagehisa. Knowing of his reputation, I eagerly sought to engage him in a bout. Indeed, he was unlike any fencers I had challenged before. His exterior was soft but he was as hard as a rock on the inside. With a spiritual respiration so intense, he was able to triumph over any opponent before the contest began. He was a truly enlightened master of swordsmanship. I engaged him countless times after our first encounter, but could never put down this almighty adversary no matter what I tried. I trained with many different opponents during the day, and meditated each evening, reflecting on the significance of respiration. When I closed my eyes and focused, I saw images of Asari with sword in hand, standing before me like a mountain. It was impossible for me to strike at him or drive this vision away."

Tesshū received guidance in Zen from a number of eminent masters such as Gannō, Seijō and Dokuon from the Sōkokuji Temple in Kyoto. But the most influential master in the course of Tesshū's training was Tekisui Giboku, the abbot of the Tenryūji Temple.

"Tekisui said to me, 'Things are good but please allow an insignificant monk to say one thing. That is, your present state is as if you are looking through spectacles. They serve to clarify your vision rather than impede it. Yet, one without bad eyesight in the first place has no need for spectacles. Not only are spectacles unnecessary but they make objects appear distorted. Such a man is better off without in order to view things in their natural state. You have already reached the periphery of what you seek. If you can remove this last remaining obstacle, you will find what you have been seeking for so long. You are a man of the sword and Zen. Once you are enlightened, you will be able to transcend concerns of death and life and possess special powers. You are now at a stage where a riddle can take you beyond the periphery. In the end, all you need is one thing – *mu* (no-thing).'

I considered this riddle very carefully day and night. It's been ten years and I still do not fully understand. I visited Tekisui again, and told him of my thoughts and he presented me with another *kōan*: 'When two flashing swords meet there is no place to escape; move on calmly, like a lotus flower in bloom in the midst of a great fire, and forcefully pierce the heavens!' I pondered this *kōan* obstinately for the next three years before realising its hidden meaning." (*Kempō to Zenri*- April, 1880.)

In this way, Tesshū immersed himself totally in his search for enlightenment. He wrote the following words in regards to calligraphy.

"When I was 11 years old I was directed by my father to go to Hida-Takayama. I practised martial arts every day, and studied calligraphy whenever I had a spare moment. There was a man named Iwasa Ittei who became famous for his skill in calligraphy. My father allowed me to study under his tutelage even though I was not yet able to write properly. Ittei gave me a volume of 1000 words that he had brushed. I copied his work diligently for a month, and finally my characters started to take form.

My father handed me a bundle of paper and instructed me to carefully write down all of the characters that I had learned. It was a little after ten o'clock in the evening. Following his suggestion, I wrote 1000 characters in 63 pages not including the date and signature. Upon completion I presented the pages to my father for inspection. It was a little before two o'clock in the early hours. My father was astonished and said to me, 'How smoothly they are written. I cannot hide my sense of disbelief. Yet, I know that you are the only one who could have written these words. The style of handwriting is undoubtedly yours. This is the paper I gave you. The characters are written so well, and I know you to be scrupulous. Do not forget this spirit and strive to master both the sword and the brush', he said to me affectionately.

My father invited Ittei the next day, and placed the pages that I brushed before him. Ittei was astounded and said, 'How striking this work is. If somebody was to see this they would never believe that it had been written by a child. It is unbelievable that he can achieve this level in such a short time of study. I am in awe of this child.' He continued his praise. 'This child is dependable and full of potential.' This encouraged me greatly....

I happened to hear that a Chinese scholar named Ō Gishi (C: Wang Xizhi) was an excellent calligrapher. I borrowed books of his calligraphy from friends, my brother-in-law, and purchased some from shops. I duplicated his scrolls whenever I had time for ten years. I also practised by copying the works of other masters. However, my level is far from proficient. All I can do is try and copy the works of the masters.

Many years ago, I went to worship at the Gokokuji Temple in Otowa. There, I happened to notice an exquisite work of calligraphy displayed in a corner. The characters were completely free of the mundane, and the brush strokes were pure and unsullied. The clouds, smoke, and the dragon looked as if they were soaring off the paper. It had an immense emotional impact on me, and when I looked at it carefully, I found that it was the work of none other than Kōbō Daishi, the patriarch of Buddhism in Japan. It is impossible to describe the magnificent beauty present in his brushwork. It impressed me more than words can express.

Henceforth, I studied various styles of brushwork written by priests and laymen, and collected whatever I could of Daishi's works. I copied them fervently, and after a number of years I finally attained a certain level of mastery, but could only ever paint a snake as opposed to a real dragon. That was in 1872 or 1873. On March 30, 1880, with my deep understanding of swordsmanship and Zen, I came to grasp the essence of calligraphy and the brush. Although I understand the secrets I am unable to explain them in words."

In 1880, Tesshū was 45 years of age. The insurmountable image he carried for 17 years of the Ittō-ryū master, Asari Yoshiaki, suddenly dissipated with this realisation, and he brimmed with energy. On May 14, he told an old acquaintance, "Chūjō, if Miyamoto Musashi himself were to come back to challenge me, I may not win, but I certainly would not lose either." Chūjō Kinnosuke (later Kageaki) was a renowned swordsman of the Shingyō-ryū and the leader of the Shinchōgumi, a band of warriors who protected the shogun.

Tesshū possessed copies of Musashi's self-portrait and his military treatise *Hyōhō Sanjūgo-kajō* (35 articles on strategy). He also reproduced Musashi's *Dokkōdō* (The path of aloneness). This attests to the extent that Tesshū was mindful of Musashi, and how he aspired to reach the same heights of mastery. His comment to Chūjō is an indication of how far he actually progressed. When he crossed swords with Tesshū, Chūjō found he was completely unable to move his arms and legs.

It is at this time that we see a change in Tesshū's calligraphy which resonated with vital energy (*ki-in seidō*). He produced many works in which he recorded the year, so it is a simple matter of comparison to verify his enlightened leap.

Asari Yoshiaki subsequently made Tesshū the successor of Ittō-ryū swordsmanship. Tesshū then established the Mutō-ryū, (School of the Sword of No-Sword). He was also certified by Tekisui as an enlightened master of Zen. He had studied Jikishin Kage-ryū swordsmanship under Kusumi Kantekisai, Hokusin Ittō-ryū under Inoue Kiyotora, and the Ittō-ryū from Asari Yoshiaki. He practised Zen under the tutelage of Gannō of the Chōtokuji Temple, Seijō of the Ryūtakuji Temple, Dokuen of the Shokokuji Temple, Kōsen of the Enkakuji Temple, and Tekisui of the Tenryūji Temple. He learned calligraphy under Iwasa Ittei, the 51st headmaster of the Jubokudō style, and under tutors of various traditions for over 30 years.

Tesshū's brushwork on page 35 is the character '*ryū*' (龍) or dragon and was written when he was 50 years of age. Considering his work resonated with *ki-in seidō* from the age of 45, this particular piece has a sense of benevolence, and demonstrates his diligence and sincerity. Tesshū continued his studies until the day he died.

"Whenever I had a chance to break from my duties each day, without fail I would use the opportunity to pursue my studies of *ken-zen-sho*. There was great demand for my work, and I would often write over 200 pieces a day."

The *Hōjō Kata* and 'Losing one's Body'

The Jikishinkage-ryū was created by Matsumoto Bizen no Kami Naokatsu of Kashima (1478-1534). In this system there are four sword forms (*kata*) called *hōjō* which teach correct cutting technique, *ki-ai* (spirit), *ma-ai* (distance and timing) and other components of combat. Each *kata* is associated with a season (spring, summer, autumn, winter), of which the characteristics of each is manifest in the movements of each form.

The first *kata*, *hassō happa*, represents spring with its smooth but rapid movements. The second *kata*, *ittō ryōdan*, corresponds to summer with its explosive movements and fiery energy. *Uten saten*, the third form, represents autumn with its varied pace and changes in direction. The final *kata* is *chōtan ichimi*, and it represents winter with its internalised spirit, and slow but firm movements. It is the most quiet and subdued of all the forms.

An important characteristic of the Jikishin Kage-ryū is not the cutting or thrusting techniques, or striking or holding down, but how it is applied to vigilant action in everyday life, even in the simple act of drinking *sake* with a friend. A good demonstration of this ideal can be found in a well-known story of how Yamada Jirōkichi, the 14th successor of the school, was awarded his teaching licence from his master Sakakibara Kenkichi. The two were walking the slippery snow-covered Kudan slope. The elderly Kenkichi lost his clog, to which

Jirōkichi immediately replaced it with his own the very instant his teacher put his foot down. This was a clear demonstration of *mu-shin* (acting without thought; state of no-mind), and demonstrated the high level of Jirōkichi's attainment in the teachings of the school, even outside the *dōjō*.

In the *hōjō kata*, *uchidachi* (teacher) has the light to his back and *shidachi* (student) moves in his shadow. In all four *kata*, *shidachi* triumphs in each encounter. This is in accordance with the philosophy of the Jikishin Kage-ryu, in which one must become the shadow (*kage*). A shadow is created when light is blocked, but cannot move of its own accord. In order to identify with the shadow, *shidachi* must face death as *uchidachi* initiates all of the attacks and moves first. Accepting or being prepared for death, the student can reach the state of "absolute self".

In the famous 18th century samurai treatise *Hagakure*, the Yamamoto Tsunetomo states, "I have found that the meaning of *bushidō* is found in death." The warrior must be prepared to bravely forfeit his life when that time has come. The passage also contains the nuance that the warrior should be devoted to the ancient way of *bushidō* (way of the warrior) by performing his duties selflessly every living moment. A later passage states "In order to master the essence of *bushidō*, you must die anew every morning and night. If you can preserve the state of death in your everyday life, you will understand the spirit of *bushidō*, and you will gain freedom. Then you will be able to fulfill your duties to your lord for the rest of your life." The *Hagakure*'s orator, Yamamoto Jōchō (Tsunetomo) studied Zen from the age of 21 under Tannen Oshō, the priest of the Kōdenji Temple. It is clear through his writings that he was influenced by Zen thought.

Hakuin (1685-1768) was a Zen master of the Rinzai-sect of the calibre said to be born only once every 500 years. This extremely influential Zen master, painter and calligrapher, inherited his discipline from Shidō Bunan (1603-1676). Bunan gained renown as a great spiritual master, and he resided in a hermitage in Koishikawa, Edo until his death. His calligraphy is exquisite, and his Zen is the act of completely and utterly nullifying the self.

Bunan was born in Sekigahara, the site of the decisive battle in the rise of Ieyasu and the Tokugawa shogunate in 1600. Amidst these unsettled times, Bunan embraced a perception of the evanescence of life. He was attracted to Zen and decided to enter the priesthood. For 30 years he studied while leading a stark and frugal life. He was finally able to solve the *kōan* "Shidō bunan yuiken kenjaku". (The ultimate path is not difficult to reach, just do not be particular.) He took the name Shidō Bunan when he was 47 years of age.

Thereafter, he left us with a legacy of poems such as "Night and day, one must use the sword of the king of Kongō to kill the self. When you are able to kill the self, you will attain salvation. The life that is left is called the Buddha." "Die while alive, and be completely dead. Then do anything you wish. All is good." Tesshū regarded Bunan's idea of the state of '*mi wo nakusu*' (losing one's body) very highly, and often discussed it with his students.

Japanese Culture and "Pursuing the Way"

Motoori Norinaga (1730-1801), a prominent scholar of the Tokugawa period, stated in *Naobi no Mitama* (Spirit of renovation) "Everything is a Way". That is, one must walk the path of truth, which ultimately means to devote the self to the Way. This entails completely negating or losing the self. When Dōgen returned from his studies in China, he said he had developed a "flexible mind", and had acquired the ability to "Think as a thing, and act as a thing."

One of the main characteristics of Japanese culture is the idea of the 'Way'; and by surrendering one's body and mind, a state of "no-mind" or *mu-shin* can be arrived at. This is precisely what lies at the root of swordsmanship, Zen, and calligraphy. In the case of *ken* and *sho*, the former uses the medium of a sword, and the latter a brush. However, it is impossible to find total freedom in movement without becoming one with the tool, and in order to achieve this, one needs to 'nullify the self'. Even in Zen, the restrictive body of the self is rejected first in order to be reawakened as the 'true self'. Not to do so would leave the individual blind to the boundless nature of the true self's existence. Judging by the superb specimens of calligraphy produced by renowned historical figures such as Kūkai, Saigyō, Sesshū, and Rikyū, it is certain that they reached this level of mastery. Their works are tremendously vibrant, almost as if they are alive and breathing.

The Void and Universal Mind

In the scroll of the "Void" (*Kū-no-maki*) in Musashi's *Gorin no sho*, it states,

> "The warrior must learn the way of strategy by studying various martial arts. Nothing should be disregarded when studying the way of the warrior. He should study tirelessly from morning to night, making sure his mind doesn't wander. He must strive to polish his mind and volition, and hone his skills to understand the two visions; looking and seeing. He should realise that the true void is where the clouds of indecision have completely scattered."

This passage is referring to the ability to distinguish between all things, and not be distracted by anything. This, according to Musashi, is the "true void". He is not inferring that the "void" is indicative of having no knowledge, or suggesting indifference to the way of the warrior. The void is very much alive and vivacious. Calligraphy is the same; the style of character, brushwork, viscosity of the ink, and quality of the paper are the first considerations. Then, all of these details must be completely forgotten as brush is put to paper for the characters to spring to life.

In the *Hanya shingyō* (S: *Prajñāpāramitā hrdaya sūtra*) this realm is called *shikisoku-zekū* – "The phenomenal being is emptiness" All existence like this is 'true form', just as the self is true only when forgotten. When the self is entirely gone,

the world then becomes the self, and everything is differentiated with no two things being the same. A life which is equal with any other life form becomes unique and discernable, and truly alive in *kūsoku-zeshiki* – "Emptiness is the phenomenal being."

In Zen, this state is often referred to as *mu* (emptiness). In the first section of the *Hekigan-roku*, Emperor Wu of Liang asked Bodhidharma, "What is the first principle of Buddhism?" Bodhidharma answered abruptly, "*Kakunen-mushō* – Vast emptiness, nothing sacred!" (*Blue Cliff Record*). From this world of emptiness, every living entity springs forth as expressed by the teaching "*muichi-motsu chū mujinzō*" – There are riches in the midst of nothing; flowers, moon, and even buildings. Here, *samadhi*, the consciousness of the experiencing "subject" becomes one with the experienced "object", the perfect state of spiritual concentration, is a key point.

Confucius said in the *Analects*, "At the age of 70, I could follow my heart's desires without overstepping the lines of rectitude." One day Confucius asked his disciples Tze-lu, Zan Yu, Kung-hsu Hwa and others about their desires. Tze-lu replied he would like to rule a large state. Zan Yu replied that he would like to make a small state prosperous. Kung-hsu Hwa replied that he would like to act as an assistant to help the ruler of the state through ritual courtesy and music. Last of all Tsang Hsi, pausing as he played on his lute, laid the instrument aside while it was still twanging, "In this, the last month of spring, with the dress of the season all complete, along with five or six young men who have assumed the cap, and six or seven boys, I would bathe in the springs, enjoy the breeze among the rain altars, and return home singing." The Master heaved a sigh of relief and said, "I give my approval to Tsang." If we apply this answer to the aforementioned *go-i*, it would correspond with *Ken-chū-tō* – the highest level where form and emptiness fully interpenetrate. A true world of '*yu*' (遊=exploration) where there are no constraints whatsoever; this is the "true void."

When Tesshū practised Zen meditation in his younger years, he was said to be so intense that scurrying mice froze when they wandered into his vicinity. In his later years, however, when he was copying sutras, mice would come and sit on his knees and shoulders. Troubled people who visited him would become so revitalised that they would not leave until the evening. When asked of the secrets of *kendō*, he always replied that the answer was with the Kannon (Bodhisattva of great compassion) in Asakusa. At the temple, there is a sign inscribed with the characters *"semui"* (giver of fearlessness – steadfast determination free of doubt). He was respected by his peers as a man who radiated energy, just like a living Buddha with a universal mind.

Chō Sanshū (1823-1895) was a famous poet and calligrapher who expressed doubt that Tesshū could possibly write five or 600 pieces of calligraphy in a single day. Tesshū retorted, "You break your bones because you are writing characters. I am simply applying ink, so there is no strain at all." In other words, he was insinuating that Chō Sanshū's mind was consciously operating when he wrote his characters. In Tesshū's case, especially in his twilight years, he was impervious to the action of brushing the characters, and what ended up on the paper was an unconscious expression of his soul. He drew an analogy to the skills required by a carpenter when shaving wood. Tool, carpenter, and beam must function together in perfect unison, just as mind, body and technique should." "When mind, body and technique are forgotten, the task proceeds effortlessly until completion."

Bunan said that from a state of absolute nothingness attained by complete and total self-annihilation, the heart that springs forth is one of "compassion, harmony, and honesty." I believe that this corresponds with what modern scientists call "universal purpose."

Tesshū's "sword of no-sword" gave people a sense of fearlessness that put them at ease. His sword was a medium for the 'Way' of *semui*. Musashi's sword pierced the "void", and his transcendence of the mundane is evident in the mysterious and boundless warmth evoked in his works. Although different in form to the works left by Zen masters such as Shidō Bunan and Fūgai Ekun, one thing they all

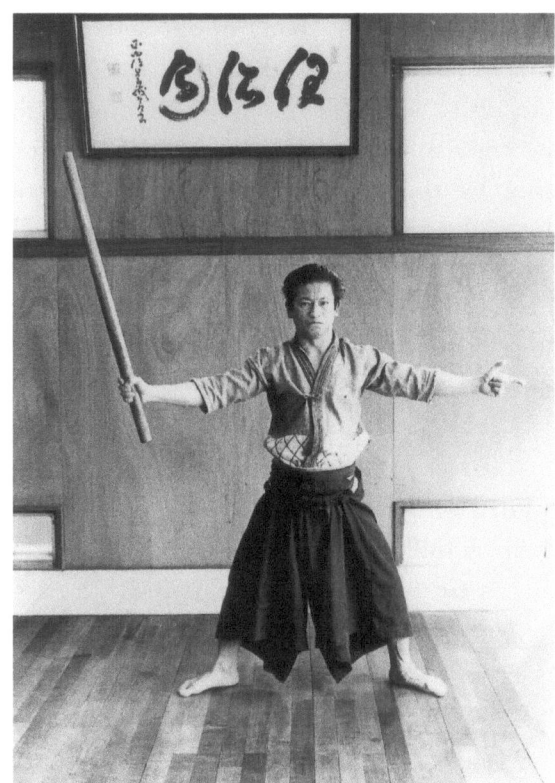

Terayama Tanchū practising the *hōjō kata*

have in common is the same fundamental 'life' emanating from them. The *ken-zen-sho* of Musashi and Tesshū exhibit enlightened qualities. Even in this age of advanced scientific and technological progress, we are still greatly attracted to such profound achievements. Although accomplished by special individuals, their legacy is an asset for all of humanity.

References

Ōmori Sōgen, *Ken to Zen* (The sword and Zen), Shunjūsha, 1966

Yamada Jirōkichi, *Nihon Kendo-shi* (The history of Japanese *kendō*), Hitotsubashi Kenyūkai, 1976

Kashima Shinden Jikishin Kage-ryu, Hitotsubashi Kenyūkai, 1976

Yokoyama *Kendō*, *Nihon Budo-shi* (The history of Japanese martial arts), Shimazu Shobō, 1991

剣・禅・書と現代

寺山　旦中

発生と成熟

　剣術の発生は、剣の創造に由来すると思われるので、その歴史は古い。が、今はその歴史的な詳細は省き、それが死の恐怖や生の不安からの脱却に生じ、そこに起因して成熟して来たことのみを、指摘するにとどめたい。

　そして、源平時代から足利期にわたっての永い戦闘の経験から、その勝敗の理法が検討されて、その理にのっとって教習法が工夫され、そこに「生死決定」としての剣術の流派が発生してきたようだ。

　その代表的なものが、西の陰流（長享1487〜1489）と、東の天真正伝神道流（文明1469〜1487）で、それから古い時代の流祖は神仏に祈願、あるいは怪獣や河童等の超人的威力の持主から、その極意を授かっているのである。このことは、甚だ興味ぶかい。

　それが、だんだんと時代と技術が進むにつれ、剣を使う主体への反省となり、上泉伊勢守の“不滅の心”さらに宮本武蔵の“厳の身”柳生流の“西江水”針ヶ谷赤雲の“無佳心”辻月丹の“一法無外”神谷伝心斎の“直心”そして山岡鐵舟の“施無畏”等は、いのちの根源を直指し、生死を覚証した、その悟境の表現だったのである。

　そのように剣術は、生死を決するわざから道に深化されてきたが、鎌倉時代の北条時宗が生死の岩頭に立って、無学祖元に参じたように、禅も生を明らめ死を明らめることが、その最大事であった。ゆえに道元禅師は「生を明らめ死を明らむるは佛家一大事の因縁なり」（『正法眼蔵』―諸悪莫作）と、喝破したのである。

　大燈国師・宗峰妙超も、禅は“己事の究明”こそが最も大切なこと、とその遺誡に示すように、それは真実の自己をつかまえ、それを生きることに外ならない。真実の自己は、百年足らず、百キログラム足らず、二メーター足らずという、限定された個体ではなく、実は無限の広がりをもつ。「盡十方界、是箇眞實人體なり、生死去來、眞實人體なり」（『正法眼蔵』―身心学道）と道元が記すように、十方に広がる身体こそが、ほんとうのからだになるのである。

　それは人間が、限りある生命と、その弱小な能力とに気づいて、何とか無限にして、絶大な力に結びつこうと永い間格闘して来た、そんな結果至り得た境地でもあった。

　それには、いま、ここに活潑々地にはたらいているそのいのちを活捉することだ、と臨済禅師は言う。「即今・目前・聴法底」（『臨済録』）に出入する「無位の真人」（『臨済録』）こそが、それだというのである。ために坐禅をし、自己をならう。禅は、すべて己れの中にあると示すからである。「自己をならふというは、自己をわするるなり」（『正法眼蔵』―現成公案）で、自己を忘れ自己なき時こそ、自己ならざるはない世界の展開である。そうするには「ただわが身をも心をもはなちわすれて、佛のいえに投げ入れ」（『正法眼蔵』―生死）なければならない。

　そのように、主に坐禅でもって己れを無にし、本来のいのちに目覚め、そしてそのいのちを主体的に生きる道として、禅は成熟して来たと言ってよかろう。

　そんな本来のいのちの躍動したものを、南斉の謝赫（479〜?）は、第一等の作品と評価した（『古畫品録』）。それは画についてであったが、中国では元来「書画一体」なので、そのことは書にも当てはまると思う。

　しかし、そこに到るまでには、例えば書聖と言われる中国の王羲之（307?〜365?）も、その手紙を集めた『自論書』に「張の精熟は人に過ぐ。・・・吾れ心を畫して精作すること。・・・」と言う。精熟とは技術面、精作とは心をこめて書いたとのことゆえ精神面、ゆえに古来書はその両面より評価し、そこに向って錬磨して来た、と言わなければならない。

　その結果、空海は書というものは「懐抱を散逸」（『性霊集』）することだと言い、黄山谷（1045〜1105）は40歳台の自分の書には「筆が無かった」と言う。そして、字中に筆があるというのは、禅者の詩に字眼という宗旨があるようなものだ（『山谷題跋』）と説く。つまり、「筆がなかった」ということは、気韻生動したところがなかった、ということになろう。

　『入木抄』（1352年成立）は、尊円親王が後光厳天皇に、書道について解説された著作である。その中には「能書の手跡は、生きたる物にて候。精霊魂魄の入りたる様に、見え候うなり」とか「いずくにも精霊有りて弱き所無し」〜とあり「この道その実を申し候えば、佛法の悟りによりおこりて、世俗の技藝に出で候」等とある。

となると、書も第一義は技術ではなく、精霊魂魄が入り、気韻生動したもの、即ち本来のいのちの躍動したものこそ、その最も大切なところ、と言ってよかろう。

よって、剣・禅の道が主に生死をのりこえるために生れ、それには自我を勦絶し、不生不滅の本来のいのちに立ち還って、そのいのちと生きる道へと成熟し、書もそんないのちの舞踏の作品を貴ぶことに気付く時、そこに貫道するものは一つのいのちだったのである。

山岡鐵舟と剣・禅・書

剣・禅・書を一如に行じた人には、柳生宗矩（1571〜1645）はじめ何人かが目につくが、ここには宮本武蔵（1582〜1645）と山岡鐵舟（1836〜1888）をとり挙げたい。

武蔵は、播磨の国の田原家に生れ、十手の名人であった無二斉の家伝継承のため、新免家の養子となったと思われる。よって、武道に生きることは、いわば彼の宿命であった。ゆえに、13歳（年齢はすべて数え）で新当流の有馬喜兵衛と戦ったのをはじめ、28・9歳のころまでに60余度の真剣勝負を行ったが、一度も負けなかった（『五輪書』）と言う。

しかし、30歳を過ぎて振り返ってみるに、今までの勝負は理に則とって勝ったのではない。たまたま相手の未熟さゆえか、偶然に理にかなうという僥倖だった、と気付いたというのである。

そして「其後なをもふかき道理を得んと、朝鍛夕練してみれば、をのづから兵法の道にあふ事、吾五十歳の比也。其より以来は尋入るべき道なくして光陰を送る。兵法の利にまかせて、諸藝諸能の道となせば、萬事において我に師匠なし」と『五輪書』の冒頭に記す。

そこには、20年間の悪戦苦闘があった。その結果、自我が滅却したに相違ない。それまで、みずから求めて来たものが、向うからやって来ておのずからの世界につきぬけた。180度の転換である。その自らの兵法の理でもってすると、諸藝道の道にもかない、師匠なくして書画や彫刻や金工等までに通じた、というのである。

勿論、やらないことは出来ないので、そういったものには子供の頃から興味もあり、その20年間の工夫錬磨中にも、多少はそれらをたしなんでいたのであろう。

そして、その理は禅の法理に照らしても、矛盾はなかった

と思われる。武蔵と禅のかかわりは、その文章が体験より成るものであることや「直心」や「吟味」等の禅的表現や、彼の作品に達磨図や布袋図といった禅画の多いことなどからしても、そのことは容易に窺われるが、特に『五輪書』の空の巻等は、それがつよい。

だいたい、兵法書が、地・水・火・風・空の5段階に整理され『五輪書』と呼ばれるようになった背景にも、禅の「五位」の影響があったであろう。

五位とは、曹洞宗の始祖の洞山良价と曹山本寂の開示になるもので、その境界を五種の位に分け、功勲五位、正偏五位、君臣五位があるが、ここには正偏五位の五つの段階を指す。それは、正中偏、偏中正、正中来、兼中至、兼中到である。

兼中到とは、兼中至の到着点で、森羅萬象あるがままに見、為すがままに行う何の変哲もない当り前のところである。十牛図なら、返本還源から入鄽垂手といったところで『五輪書』の空の巻は、これに当るであろう。

武蔵は「今此書を作るといへども、佛法儒道の古語をもからず」と、その冒頭にことわっているので、そんなものを十分に消化し、解り易く表現したものに相違ない。その修禅と確証は、34歳も年下の春山和尚ではなく、大渕和尚によったものと思われるのである。

鐵舟は、7・8歳のころ、母・磯に習字を学んだ。その中に「忠孝」なる文字があり、その意を問うた。よって母は、「忠」とは主君に仕えて心の正しきこと。「孝」とは、親にそのように仕えることと教えた。すると鐵太郎少年は「母様は、常にその道を守られていますか」と問う。が、母はしばらく黙していたが、そのうち涙を落として、「おう、鐵よ！自分は常々そう心がけてはいるけれども、私はつまらぬ女ゆえ、なかなかそうはできなくて残念に思う。お前はどうか、それが出来る人間になっておくれ」と慈訓された。このことを「余が神心に浸み渡れり」と、後年鐵舟は記している（「父母の教訓と剣と禅とに志せし事」）。

加うるに、13歳のころ父・高福から「いやしくも身を武門にゆだねる者は、忠孝の志ゆめゆめ忘るべからず」それには「形に武藝、心に禅理の修練が第一」と諭された。「故に余は爾後、この二道に心を潜めんと欲するに至れり」と自書（元治元年甲子正月十日）している。鐵舟、時に29歳であった。よって、鐵舟の人となりの形成の原点はここにあり、その一生は「忠孝」の実践だった、と言っても過言ではない。

ここで少し、若いころからの鐵舟の剣・禅・書の修行ぶり
を、彼の語るところに見てみよう。先ず、剣については、

　　全少壮ノ頃ヨリ武藝ヲ学ビ、心ヲ禅理ニ潜ムルコト
　　久シ矣。感ズル所ハ必ラズ形ニ試ミ、以テ今日ニ至
　　ル。年九歳ノ頃、初メテ剣法ヲ久須美閑適齋ニ学ビ、
　　続イデ井上清虎、千葉周作、或ハ、斉藤、桃井等ニ受
　　ケ、其他試合スル事、其数幾千万ナルヲ知ラズ。如斯
　　ニシテ刻苦精思スル事凡二十年。然レドモ、更ニ其人
　　ニ遇フ能ハズ。適々一刀流ノ達人浅利又七郎義明ト
　　云フ人アリ、奥平家剣法師範中西子正ノ次男ニシテ、
　　伊藤一刀斎景久ノ伝統ヲ継ギ頗ル上達ノ人ト云フ。
　　余之ヲ聞キ喜ビ、行キテ試合ヲ乞フ。果シテ世上流
　　行スル所ノ剣法ト大イニ其趣ヲ異ニスルモノアリ、外
　　柔ニシテ内剛ナリ、精神ヲ呼吸ニ凝ラシ、勝機ヲ未撃
　　ニ知ル。真ニ明眼ノ達人ト云フベシ。是ヨリ試合スル
　　ゴトニ、遠ク其不及ヲ知ル、爾来、修行不怠ト雖モ、浅
　　利ニ可勝方法アラザルナリ。是ヨリ後昼ハ諸人ト試合
　　ヲナシ、夜ハ獨リ坐シテ其呼吸ヲ精考ス。眼ヲ閉ヂテ
　　専念呼吸ヲ凝ラシ、想ヒ浅利ニ対スルノ念ニ到レバ、
　　彼忽チ余ガ剣ノ前ニ現ハレ、恰モ山ニ対スルガ如シ。
　　眞ニ當ル可カラザルモノトス。

と。さらに禅は、はじめは芝村長徳寺の顧翁や龍澤寺の
星定、あるいは京都相国寺の独園らの諸師に参じたが最も
益を被ったのは、天龍寺の滴水老師であった。そのことを彼
は、こう記す。

　　滴水ノ曰ク、善哉言ヤ、然レドモ愚僧等ノ道ヲ以テ包
　　シナク一言スレバ、貴下ノ現在ハ恰モ眼鏡ヲ隔テテ物ヲ
　　視ルガ如シ。眼鏡素ヨリ明白ニシテ、多分ノ視力ヲ妨ゲ
　　ズト雖モ、本来肉眼ニ一点ノ疾ナキ人ハ、如何ナル眼鏡
　　ト雖モ、尋常物ヲ視ルニ於テ之ヲ用フルノ要ナキノミナ
　　ラズ、用フレバ變則ナリ、用ヒザルヲ以テ自然トス。貴下
　　ノ現在ハ既ニ此ノ境ニ達セリ。若シ一度此ノ障物ヲ去
　　ル事ヲ得バ、忽チ御所望ノ極底ニ達スルコトヲ得ベシ。
　　況ヤ貴下ハ剣禅兼ネ至ルノ人ナリ。一朝豁然トシテ悟
　　道セラレナバ殺活自在神通遊化ノ境ニ到ラン、ナゾトテ
　　深ク余ヲ励マシ、且ツ曰ク、要ハ唯ダ無ノ一字ノミト。

　　余ハ此ノ公案ヲ受ケテ日夜精考スル事、約十年
　　ニ近シト雖モ猶釋然タラザルモノアリ。二度滴水ニ
　　参ジテ所存ヲ述ブ。滴水又更ニ公案ヲ挙ゲテ曰ク
　　両　刃　交　鋒　不　須　避、好手還同火裏蓮、宛然
　　自　　在　　衝　　天　　氣ト。以テ余ニ其思考ヲ促ス。余其
　　句ノ頗ル興味アルヲ感ジ、紳ニ私書シテ以テ考察具
　　サニ至ル事約三年ノ久シキニ渉ル。（以上「剣法ト禅
　　理」明治13年4月自記）

と、徹底このように参じて、自我を勦絶したのである。そして、
書についてはこう記す。

　　余年十一歳の頃、愚父朝右衛門に從て、飛騨国高
　　山の邑に在り。毎日武藝を学び、暇あれば習字を事と
　　す。折柄当地の人にして岩佐一亭なるもの書を以て鳴
　　る。是を以て愚父余をして書法を一亭に学ばしむ。余
　　未だ漢字を書するの法を知らず。而して一亭は直に千
　　字文一巻を認めて余に授く。余之を真似る事約一月、
　　漸く字形をなすに至る。是に於いて愚父は美濃半紙を
　　余に授けて曰く、汝従来修得したる所の文字を此紙に
　　清書す可しとの仰せ有之。時刻は夜の口二更（午後十
　　時）強なりし。因て余は直に筆を採り、楷書にして全千
　　字、紙数六十三葉、年月署名をなしと以て之を愚父の
　　面前に供す。時に夜半三更（午前2時）弱。愚父驚き曰
　　く。汝の此書を成す余りに速やかなるは、一応吾　れ
　　之を疑ふに似たれども、此筆跡や汝の書に相違なく、
　　此紙や吾れさきに汝に授けたるものに相違なし。汝が
　　成蹟頗る可なり。汝は正直の奴なり。爾後猶此心を忘
　　れず文武共に怠る勿れとて、深く余を愛し給へり。而し
　　て愚父翌日直に一亭を招き、出して之を示す。一亭驚
　　き曰く、成程妙なり。他人之を見なば、よもや児童の筆
　　跡とは思ふまじ。殊に短時間の成業には吾れまた驚く
　　に耐へたり。此児や恐るべし。此児や頼母しとて、亦深
　　く余を励まさる。…偶々聞く、支那人王義之なる者頗
　　る書に巧なりと。故に余は其字帖を同僚或は義兄泥
　　舟に借り、或いは書店に購い間暇を得れば筆を執っ
　　て之を真似る事凡そ十余年。時に或は諸名家の字帖
　　を並べて彼是参習したる事なきにあらず。然れども余
　　が志の不忠不誠、到底真似だに及ばざるなり。

余嘗て慶応の昔、音羽護国寺に参す。時隅々堂殿の一隅に、書幅の懸掲せらるるを拝す。字体脱俗、筆法邪なし。恰も雲煙龍飛するが如し。轉々敬服の感に耐えざらしむ。
咫尺して拝観すれば、嗟呼是れ正しく聖佛弘法大師の御手蹟なり。余は其の筆意の妙趣、口之を状すべからずと雖も、日夜欽望の念止む能はず、爾来僧俗諸先輩に請ふて大師の御手跡を集むる事幾数種。暇毎に日夜拝写すること数年。漸くにして虎を猫に形作るの境に達せり。（犬を描かずして幸なり。）時は明治五・六年の頃なり。

と。そして、

明治13年3月30日、余剣禅の二道に感ずる処ありしより、諸方皆揆一なるを以て、書亦其筆意を変ずるに至れり。然れども是等端的の呼吸に至りては、余自ら省悟するのみにて、言之を状すべきものなし。

と、つけ加えているのである。明治13年は鐵舟45歳で、それまでに実に17年間覆いかぶさっていた、一刀流の師・浅利義明の幻影が消え、大いなるエネルギーに満たされた。ためか、その1ヵ月半後の5月14日に、彼はこんなことを言っている。「中條さん、儂は宮本武蔵が出て来ても、勝つことは出来ずとも負けはせぬ」（『山岡鐵太郎年譜』―村上康正編）と。中條とは、中條金之助のち景昭と称し、新徴組の隊長となった心形流の達人。その後静岡県金谷ヶ原に旧幕の壮士の一団をひきいて、開墾に従事していた。
鐵舟は、武蔵の肖像画や『兵法三十五ヶ条』の写しを所持し、晩年「独行道」を自写していた。それほど武蔵が念頭にあり、武蔵を追いかけて来たと思われるが、遂に"勝つこともできぬが負けもせぬ"という境地に達したのである。それは"相ぬけ"と言うべきであろうか。その時、中條は手も足も出なかったという（『武道の研究』―加藤完治）。
しかもその折、鐵舟の書は筆意が一変した。いわゆる、書も無法につきぬけ「気韻生動」したのである。書とは、そういうものである、ということを銘記せねばならない。鐵舟には、沢山の揮毫があり、その中には年齢の入ったものもかなりあるので、このことは明白である。（詳しくは小著『鐵舟と書道』巌南堂書店刊参照）

そしてこの時、県は浅利義明より一刀流を継承・無刀流につきぬけ、禅は滴水老師の印可を得て、無礙自在となったのである。そこを彼は、鐵舟流と言うが、そこに到る前は剣は心影流の久須美閑適斎・北辰一刀流の井上清虎・一刀正伝の浅利義明らに、禅は長徳寺の願翁・龍沢寺の星定・相国寺の独園・円覚寺の洪川・天龍寺の滴水らに、書は入木道の51世・岩佐一亭に、それぞれ伝統の師について刻苦精励すること、およそ30年であった。このことを、見逃してはならない。
35頁は、50歳ころの「龍」字であるが、鐵舟の書は45歳で気韻生動した上に、さらにこのような柔らかさと温情味が加わり、その真面目を発揮していくのである。
その後の鐵舟は、

爾後公務の暇を得る毎に剣・禅・書は殆ど一日も怠りたる事なし。就中書幅の如きは、常に諸方の人士需め来るもの其幾百千人なるを知らず。鮮やきも一日書するもの額面掛幅を交えて二百葉を下る事甚稀なり。・・・（「書法について」明治18.12.30誌す）

だったのである。

法定と身をなくす

直心影流は、鹿島の人・松本備前守尚勝（のち改め政元・松本は杉本との説もあり。1478～1534）の創始になるという。その基本に「法定」という組太刀がある。それは春夏秋冬の4本から成り、主に太刀筋、気合、間合等を学ぶ。
一本目の「八相発破」は春季発陽の伸び伸びとした気勢で発し破ることを勤め、二本目の「一刀両断」は、夏季炎天、焼くが如き猛烈の気合を全身に充実させ、間・髪を容れない勢いで勤める。さらに三本目の「右転左転」は、秋季粛殺の気勢で、無窮の変化を勤め、最後の「長短一味」は、冬季陰蔵に象り、精神の昇降自在を内修し、業は最も静かに勤めるのである。
直心影流の剣道で大事なことは、切るとか突く、あるいは打つとかおさえる、といった剣のやりとりにあるのではなく、例えば酒のくみ交わし等の、日常生活の中にあるのだ、ということになろう。事実、一徳斎・山田次朗吉が師の第14代直心影流継承者・榊原鍵吉から免許されたのは、雪の九段坂で足

をすべらした師の足下に、間髪を入れずに自分の下駄をさし入れた時だった。道場内の、出来ごとではなかったのである。

さらに"生れてから後身についた知識や小手先藝を除いていけば、本来具有しているところの、清く明るいいのちが蘇る"というのも、このことと別ではなかろう。

法定は一太刀一太刀が相手を切るのではなく、常に己の真中心を切る。ゆえに、いつでも臍が真直ぐ前を向き、半身（はんみ）というものがない。このことも「後来習態の容形を除き、本来清明の恒体に復する」具体的修行方法ではあるまいか。

この4本の組太刀は、打太刀が光を背にした物体とすれば、仕太刀はその影であるが、4本ともに仕太刀が勝つようになっている。ということは、影になることが直心影流の主眼と思う。影は、光りが当れば即生ずるが、絶対に進むことはない。そんな影になり切るには、いわゆる死に切らないと無理だからである。真に死に切ったら、絶対主体ということであろう。

『葉隠』の冒頭「武士道といふは、死ぬ事と見付けたり」は、死ぬべき時にはいさぎよく死ぬことには相違ないが、武士道という古来の道の中に己れを没入することでもあろう。でなければ、その数行あとに「毎朝毎夕、改めては死に改めては死に、常住死身になりて居る時は、武道に自由を得、一生越度なく、家職を仕果すべきなり」の文章は必要ないと思われるからである。

葉隠の口述者・山本常朝は、洞門の僧・高伝寺の湛然和尚に深く帰依し、21歳でその血脈を受けていた。よって、そんな考え方は、禅から来ているに相違ない。と、いうのは、500年に一人と言われる済門の白隠禅師（1685〜1768）の法の上の祖父に当たる人に至道無難（1603〜1676）がいるが、彼の書はすばらしく、しかもその禅は、徹底身をなくすことにあったからである。

無難は、関ヶ原の宿屋の生れであったが、世の変遷を観て無常観をいだき、禅にあこがれて出家したいと思っていた。そこへたまたま、都へ往来の愚堂国師に寄っていただき、親しく禅要を問うようになった。そして30年ほど修行して、直（じき）に無一物となり、さらに「至道無難、唯嫌諫択（ゆいけんけんじゃく）」の公案を透過して、名実ともに至道無難禅師となったのが、47歳の時という。

そして、彼はこう記し、こう詠う。「日夜、金剛王の宝剣を揮って、切に此身を殺すべし。

此身亡ぶときは、自然に大解脱大自在の場に到らずということ

と無し」と。"ひたすらに身は死にはてていき残る　ものをほとけと名はつけにけり""いきながら死人となりてなりはてて　思いのままにするわざぞよき"と。

この、ゆったりと、どっしりとして、しかし凛としてスケール大きく、温潤極まりない書は、徹底身をなくしたそんな無一物のところから、湧き出たいのちによるものであろう。ゆえにこの書は、いつ見ても斬新で、魅力がつきない。不生不滅の、無限のいのちの産物だからと思うのである。鐵舟も、彼の「身をなくす」ことを高く評価し、しばしば門人にそのことを語ったらしい。

日本文化と「ものにゆく道」

寸心居士・西田幾多郎は「日本文化の問題」（『西田幾多郎全集』第12巻）の冒頭で、まず日本精神は「朝日に匂ふ山桜花」のように、公明正大でなければならない、と指摘した。次いで、本居宣長の「其はただ物にゆく道こそ有りけれ」（『直昆霊（なおびのみたま）』）を挙げ、それは物の真実にゆく意であり、そのことは結局己れを尽すことだ、と説いている。

さらに己れを尽すことは、自己が絶対的に否定され、なくなることでなければならない、とつけ加えた。そして道元禅師が中国より帰朝された時「われ柔軟心を得たり」と言われたという、その柔軟心もこれで、それは「物となって考え物となって行うこと」だとも、解説されたのである。

日本文化の特徴が「ものにゆく道」であり、それは己れを尽し無心になることだとすれば、剣・禅・書の極意は、全くその通りと言わなければならない。

剣や書が、刀や筆という媒体物を使う以上、その物と一体とならなければ、それらは自在には使えない。物と一体となるには、今まで観て来たように、己れを無にすることだった。禅も、生まれたままのこの有限の個体をそのまま肯定するのではなく、一度絶対否定して蘇（よみがえ）るのでないと、無限大の真実の自己を生きることは出来なかった。言うまでもなく、空海や西行、雪舟や利休らの立派な書を遺した人達は、皆そんな人達だったのである。その書が、深く生きたのも当然だった。

実の空と宇宙意思

武蔵は『五輪書』空の巻で、「武士は兵法の道を慥（たしか）に覚へ、其外武藝を能（よく）つとめ、武士のおこなふ道、少しもくらからず、

心のまよふ所なく、朝々時々におこたらず、心意二つの心をみがき、観見二つの眼をとぎ、少もくもりなく、まよひの雲の晴れたる所こそ、實の空としるべき也」という。何もかもわきまえていて、少しもそれにと捉われないところが"まことの空"だというのである。

　物を知らないとか、武士の道をわきまえない、といった空無の頑空ではなく、活きたはたらきの出来る空である。書をかく時なども、まったくそれと同じで、字のくずし方や筆の使い方、さらに墨の濃さや紙の質等、すべて心得ていて、その上でそれら一切を忘れてまっさらの所から筆を揮うのでなければ、活きた書は書けない。

　般若心経では、そんな世界を「色即是空」という。すべてこの存在は、そのまま実態がない。自己を忘じた世界が、そうである。完全に自己がなくなれば、実は世界が自己で、森羅万象ことごとく差別であり、同じものは二つとない。平等のいのちが、そのまま差別の現実世界で「空即是色」とよみがえるのである。

　禅では、そこを「無」という場合が多い。『碧巌録』の第一則で、梁の武帝が「如何なるかこれ聖諦第一義」—禅の最も大事な事は何か？との問いに「廓然無聖」—カラリッとして何もない、と応えた達磨大師の心も、それであろう。その絶対無の世界から「無一物中無盡蔵」、花有り月有り楼台有り」と、そこから何もかもが、そのはたらきとして湧き出てくるのである。その三昧から発するところが、キイーポイントだ。

　孔子は「七十にして心の欲する所に従って、矩を喩えず」（『論語』—為政篇）と言った。ある時孔子が、門人の子路・冉有・公西華らに向って各人の希望を聴いたことがある。子路は大国を統治したいと述べ、冉有は理財をもって小国を富ませたいと答えた。公西華は礼楽をもって国を助けたいと言った。曽参の父・曾皙は名を点というが、それまで弾いていた琴を置いて「暮春、春服すでに成り、冠者五六人、童子六七人、沂に浴し、舞雲に風じ、詠じて帰らん」（『論語』—先進篇）とつぶやいた。晩春のころ、さっぱりとした春着にきがえ、気の合った若者数人と一緒に温泉にでもつかって、歌でもうたいながらぶらつきたい、とのことであろう。これをきいた孔子が「点にくみせん」と讃成した、というのである。「五位」でいうなら、さしずめ「兼中到」で、何のへんてつもないあるがままのところゆえ「遊」の世界とでも呼ぶべきであろう。そこが「実の空」と思うのである。

　鐵舟の坐禅は、若いころは猛烈で、それまで騒いでいたねずみが、ピタリと静まったという。しかし晩年は、写経するひざや肩にねずみが戯れ、悩みや苦しみがあって尋ねて来た人たちが、皆いやされて、夜ふけまで帰らなかった。剣道の極意を問うと、「浅草の観音様に預けてある」と答えるのが常であった。そこには「施無畏」という大額が今でも掲げられているが、鐵舟の晩年はまさに人々に安心を与える、生き仏だったのである。

　書の方でも、一日5・6百枚も書けるはずがないと疑って来た長三洲（1823～1895）に「長さんは字を書くのだから骨が折れるが、おれは墨を塗るのだからわけのない話だ」と言っている。長三洲が書をかく時には、文字を書くという念があったが、晩年の鐵舟には、それすらもなく、ただすらすらと己れの心を写すのみだったのであろう。彼は「大工鉋の秘術」にこう記す。仕上げの鉋は、鉋と人と柱の心体業の三つが一所にはたらかねばならないが、そのこつは「心体業の三つを忘れて只すらすらと行く所にあり」と。

　そのように、この有限なる自我を一度大死一番絶対否定して、何もない絶対無の世界から湧出する心のはたらきは「第一、慈悲なり、和なり、直也」と、無難はいう。それは今日科学者の言う「宇宙意思」と言ってもよいものであろうか。

　鐵舟の剣が、人に安心を与えるところの「施無畏」の道となり、武蔵の剣が実の空につきぬけ、その作品が温潤極まりないものとなり、無難や風外らの作品も姿形こそ違っても、底を流れるいのちは、まったく一つのものだったのである。

　よって、武蔵や鐵舟らの剣・禅・書のいきついたところはそんな世界で、科学技術万能の時代とはいえ、その境地は限りない魅力を呈し、それは個人の到達したところとはいえ、人類共有の財産と思うのである。

参考文献
『日本剣道史』
『鹿島神傳直心影流』山田次朗吉著
『日本武道史』横山健堂著
『剣と禅』大森曹玄著

Sho

CALLIGRAPHY

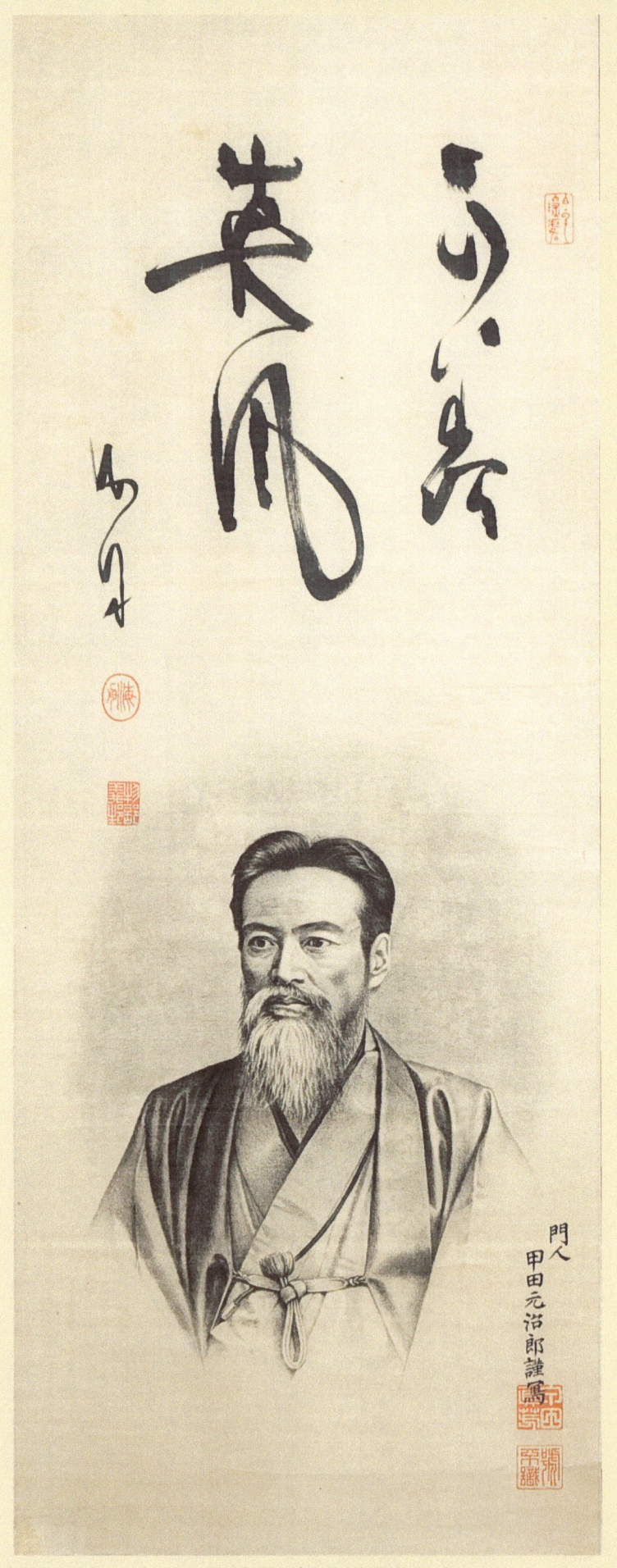

Katsu Kaishū (1823-1899)
Portrait of Yamaoka Tesshū (inscription in cursive script) 1885. Charcoal pencil drawing, and engraving and *sumi* ink on silk 104cm × 47cm.

正に英風を羨む

海舟

Masa ni eifū o urayamu   Kaishū

Truly a gifted person to be envied. Kaishū.

This formal portrait of Tesshū was drawn with reverence by Kōda Ganjirō, one of Tesshū's disciples. He has inscribed his name in regular script in the bottom right hand corner. The inscription in cursive script at the top is by Katsu Kaishū, revealing his admiration for Tesshū. The three *shū* of the Bakumatsu period were Yamaoka Tesshū, Katsu Kaishū and Takahashi Deishū. Each took the character *shū* as the second element of their formal layman name. Kaishū literally means ocean boat. All three were deeply versed in the Chinese classics, calligraphy, poetry and the martial arts.

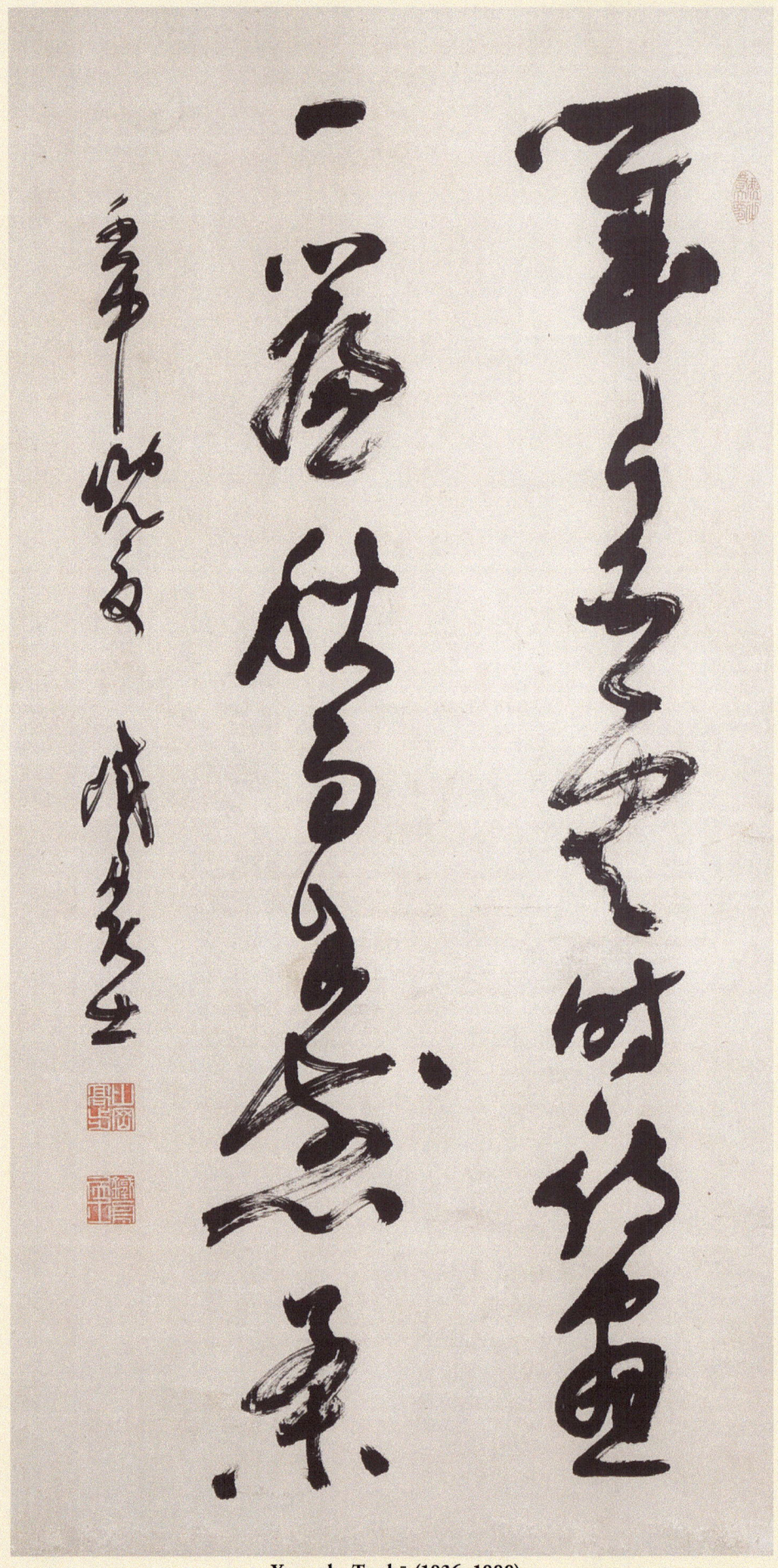

Yamaoka Tesshū (1836–1888)
Three line saying (cursive script) 1873. *Sumi* ink on paper 112cm × 55cm.

幾片白雲時待畫
一簾秋雨自煎茶
壬申晩夏鉄舟居士

Ikuhen no hakuun toki ni ga o machi Ichiren no shu'u mizukara cha o niru　　Jinshin banka　Tesshū koji

Groups of white clouds, waiting to be painted.

As the autumnal rain falls, I boil tea.

Tesshū koji, late summer.

This calligraphy was written by Tesshū at the age of 37. The signature, which is just above the seals in the left-hand column, is technically adequate but lacks the vitality and refinement of Tesshū's calligraphy after he attained enlightenment at the age of 45.

居士, or '*koji*' (sanscrit '*upsaka*'), is a title added to the name of an active Buddhist layman.

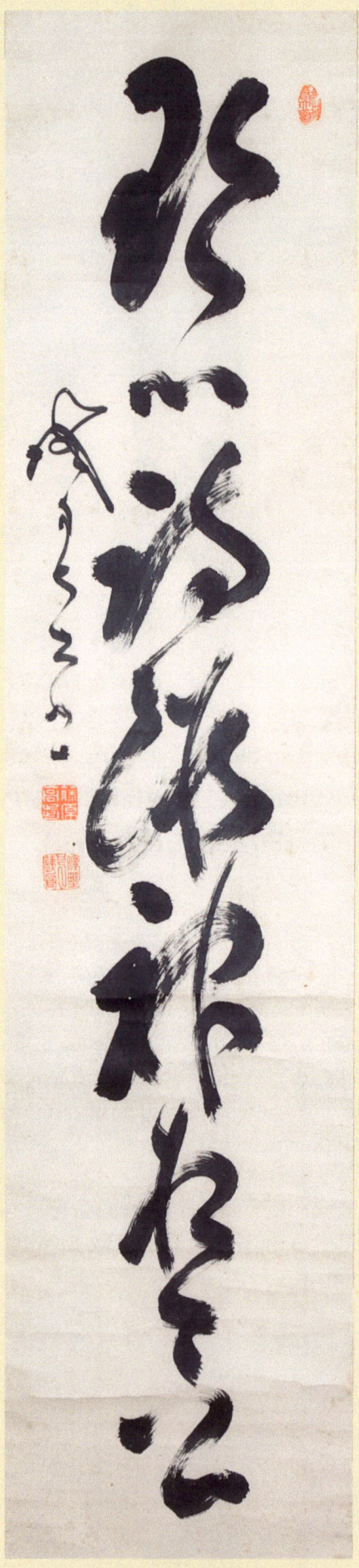

Yamaoka Tesshū (1836–1888)
One line saying (cursive script) 1887. *Sumi* ink on paper 135cm × 32cm.

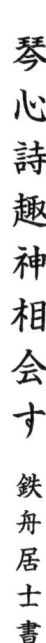

琴心詩趣神相会す　鉄舟居士書

Kinshin shishu shin ai esu　Tesshū koji sho

Music and poetry - a creation of the gods.
Written by Tesshū koji.

On March 30, 1880, at the age of 45, Tesshū was enlightened to the inner truth of Zen and swordsmanship. This was accompanied by a marked change in the quality of his calligraphy. In this work written towards the end of his life, the signature is lucid and elegant, seemingly formed with a power beyond human strength.

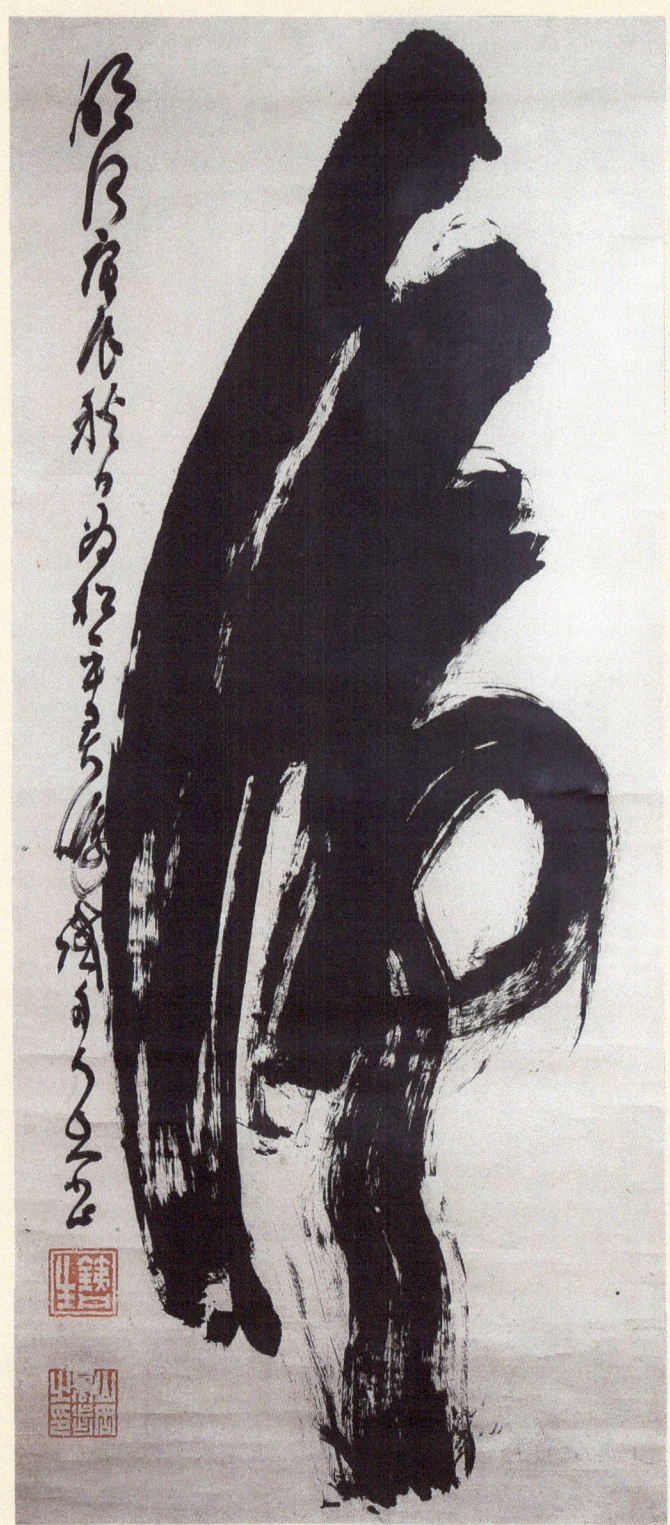
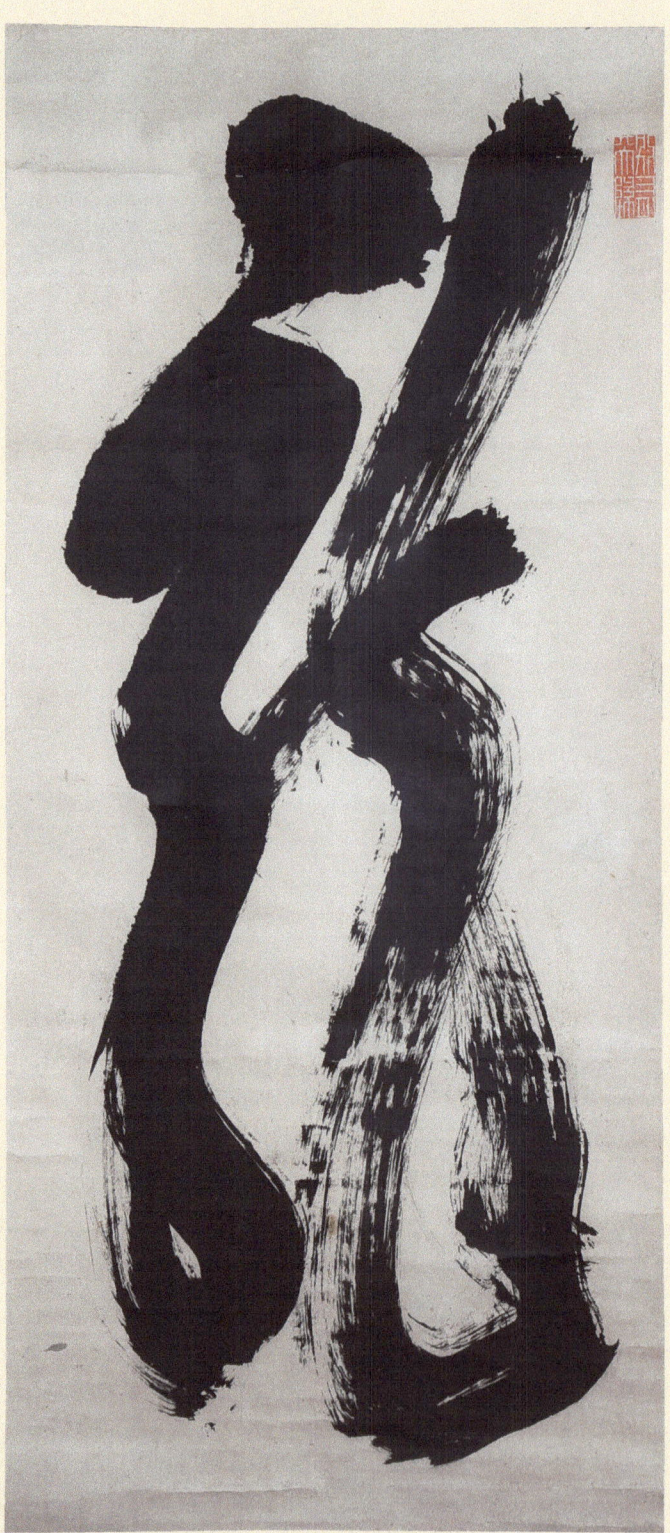

Yamaoka Tesshū (1836–1888)
Dragon and Tiger (cursive script) 1880. *Sumi* ink on paper 135.5cm × 58cm × 2.

虎　　　龍

明治庚辰秋日松平君の職のため　鉄舟居士書

Ryū　　　Ko　　Meiji kōshin shujitsu Matsudaira kun no shoku no tame ni　　Tesshū koji sho

Dragon and Tiger.

Thirteenth year of Meiji, autumn.

Written by Tesshū koji at the request of Lord Matsudaira in the autumn of Meiji 13.

This work dates from the autumn of 1880, about six months after Tesshū experienced enlightenment under the guidance of Tekisui Giboku of the Tenryūji Temple in Kyoto. The brush strokes of the signature, above the seals to the left, are vibrant and powerful. The calligraphy overflows with energy, almost as if Tesshū himself 'became' the dragon and tiger as he wielded his brush.

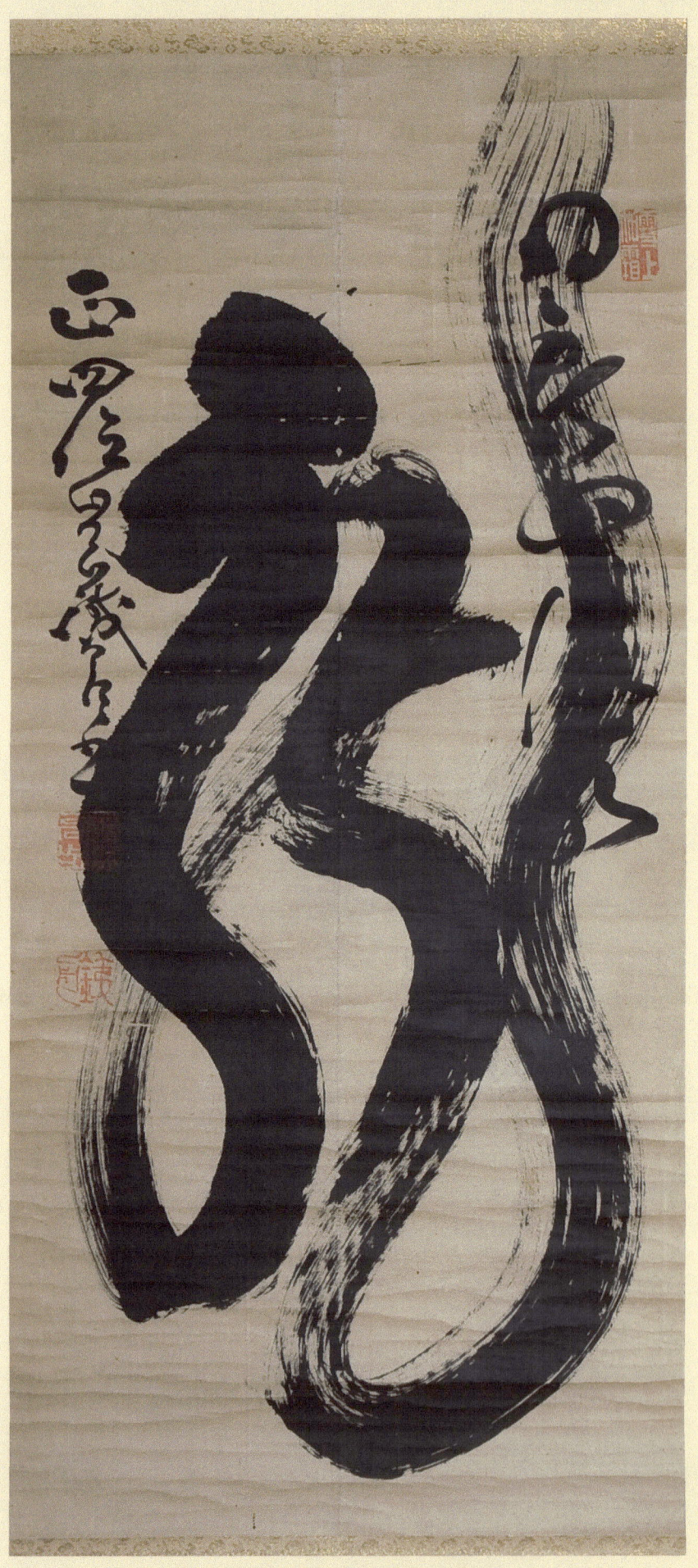

Yamaoka Tesshū (1836–1888)
Dragon (cursive script) 1885. *Sumi* ink on paper 130cm × 56cm.

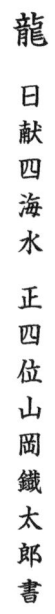

龍

日献四海水　正四位山岡鐵太郎書

Ryū   Hi ni shikai no mizu o kenzu   Shōshii Yamaoka Tetsutarō sho

Dragon.

Offering the water of the four seas to the sun.

Written by Yamaoka Tetsutarō, Senior Fourth Court Rank.

Tesshū wrote this calligraphy at the age of 50, five years after he experienced enlightenment. The initial mark at the top left has a splatter of ink, indicating the tremendous energy with which the brush hit the paper.

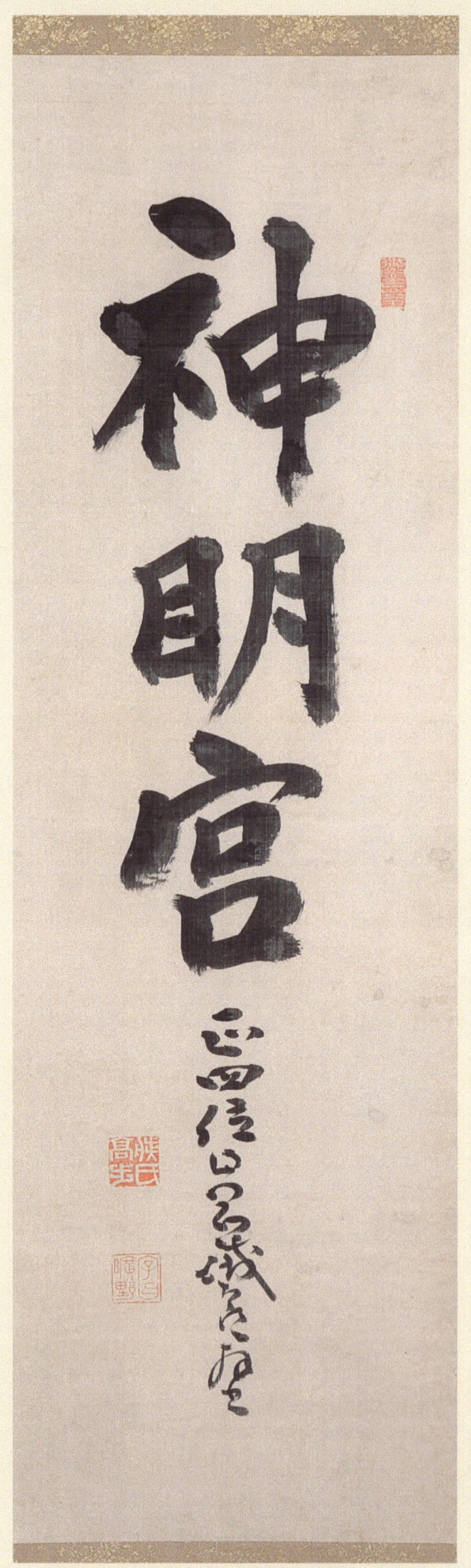

Yamaoka Tesshū (1836–1888)
One line saying (regular script) 1885. *Sumi* ink on silk 90cm × 29cm.

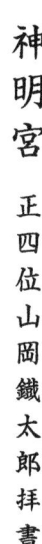

神明宮

正四位山岡鐵太郎拜書

Shinmeigū   Shōshii Yamaoka Tetsutarō haisho

Shrine of the Deity.
Brushed by Yamaoka Tetsutarō, Senior Fourth Court Rank.

Yamaoka Tesshū's commonly used name
was Tetsutarō, meaning 'iron boy'. His
formal layman's name 'Tesshū' means
'iron boat'. This calligraphy is written in
regular script, which is the form of script
most commonly used in Japan today.

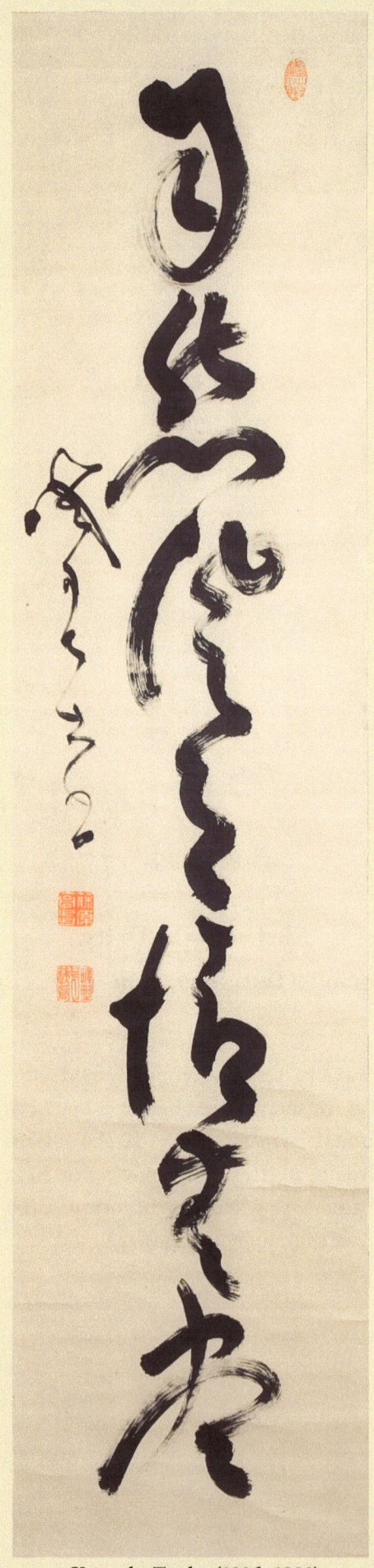

Yamaoka Tesshū (1836–1888)
One line saying (cursive script) 1885. *Sumi* ink on paper 137cm × 31cm.

自然の風月情尽きること無し 鉄舟居士書

Jinen no fūgetsu jō tsukiru koto nashi   Tesshū koji sho

Moon and breeze in nature, the feeling is inexhaustible.
Written by Tesshū koji.

This calligraphy, like many in this display, is written in cursive script. Unlike regular script, whereby characters are written neatly and independently, the forms tend to flow together in an unbroken line.

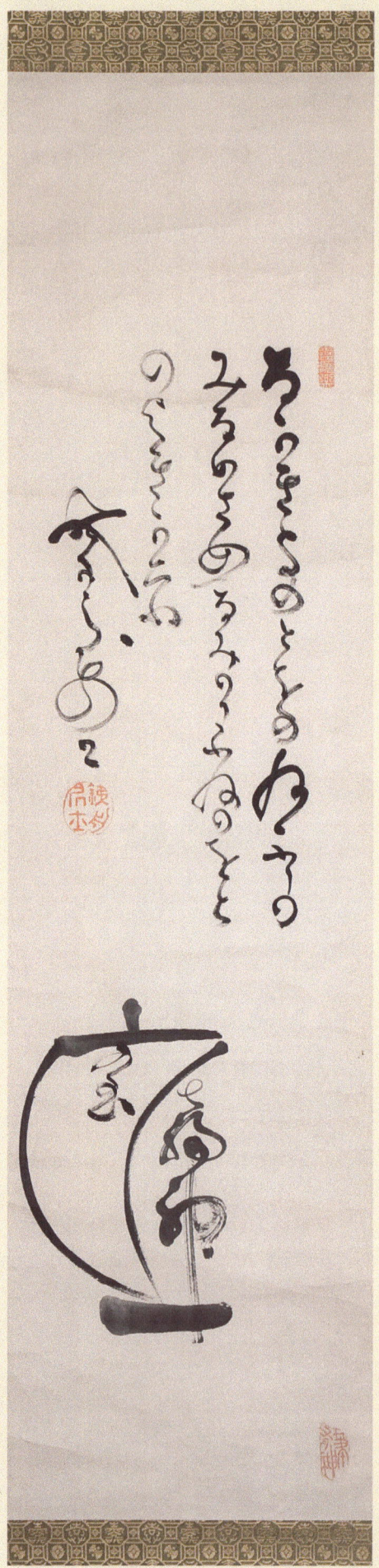

Yamaoka Tesshū (1836–1888)
Treasure ship of the Seven Gods of Good Fortune (with inscription in *kana* and cursive script) 1885. *Sumi* ink on paper 128cm × 33cm.

なばきよの　とをのねぶりの
みなめざめ　なみのりふねの
をとのよきかな

鉄舟高歩書

Nagaki yo no Tō no neburi no Mina mezame Naminori fune no Oto no yoki kana   Tesshū kōho sho

**After a long night, all the gods awake from their slumber,
stirred by the sound of waves striking against the boat.
Written by Tesshū kōho.**

This 31 syllable *waka* poem reads the
same backwards or forwards. 高歩, or
'*kōho*', was a pen name used by Tesshū.

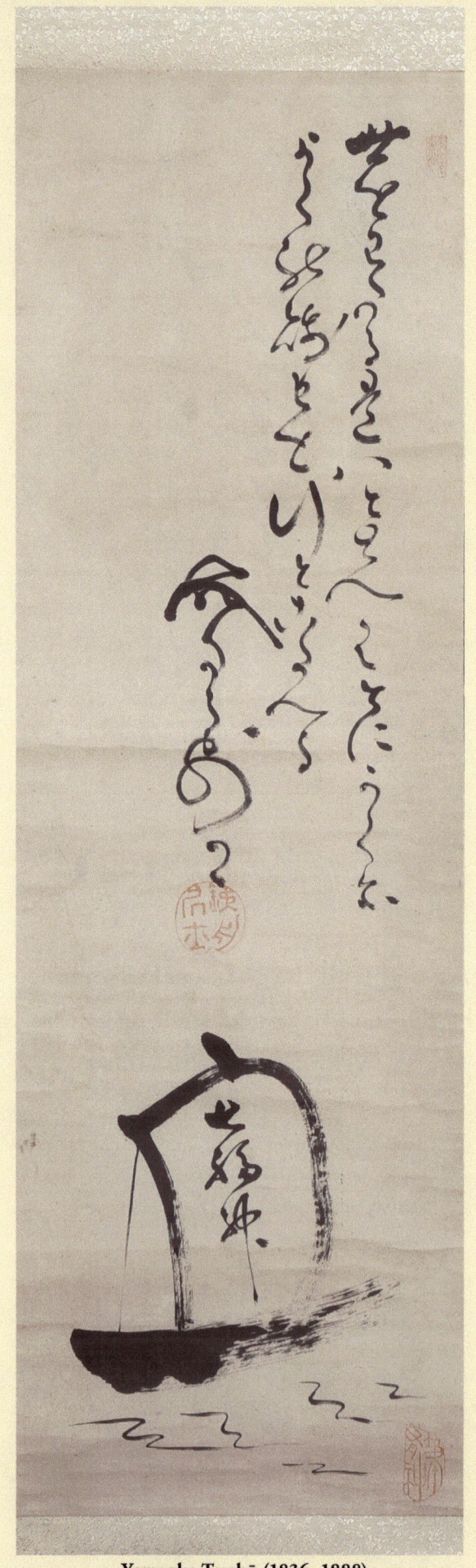

Yamaoka Tesshū (1836–1888)
Treasure ship (with inscription in *kana* and cursive script) 1885. *Sumi* ink on paper 94cm × 29cm.

世を王たる　道はとへ者　と尓かく尓
よく能賎せを行と古たえる

鉄舟高歩書

Yo o wataru Michi wa toeba Tonikaku ni Yoku no asase o Yuke to kotaeru   Tesshū kōho sho

If someone asks the way to cross over this world,
tell them – pass through the shallows of our desires.
Written by Tesshū kōho.

Cursive script was further adapted and simplified by the Japanese to create the *hiragana* syllabary, which represents particles and adjectival and verbal inflections.

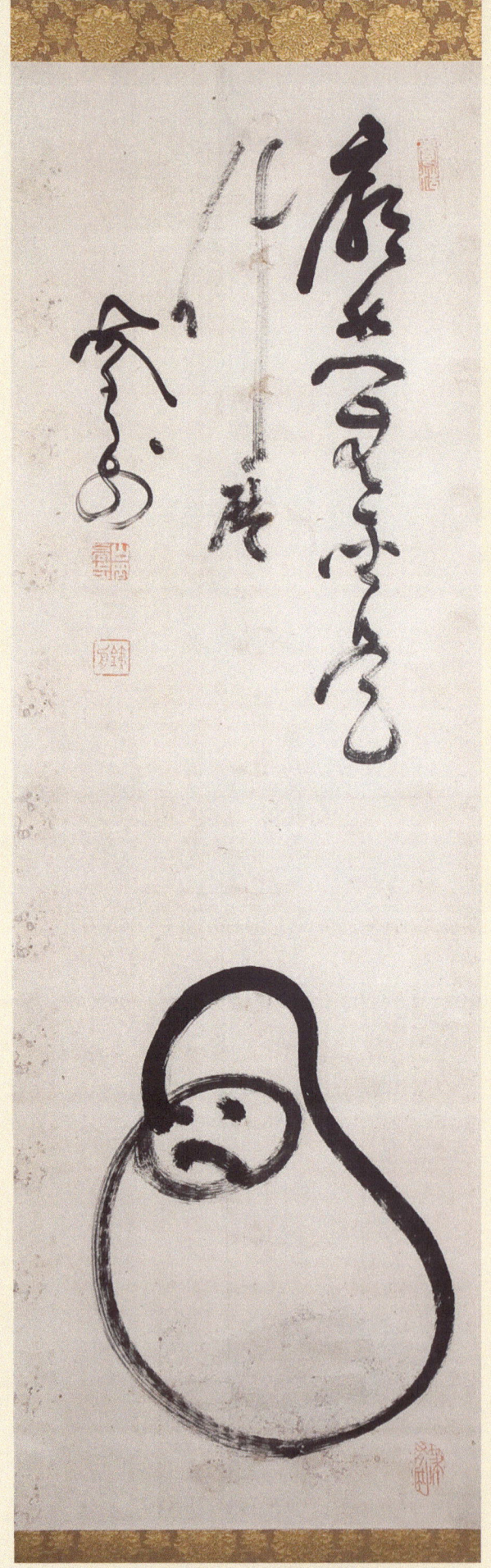

Yamaoka Tesshū (1836–1888)
Snow Daruma (with inscription in cursive script) 1885. *Sumi* ink on paper 120cm × 30cm.

廓
然
無
聖
是
什
麼

鉄
舟
高
歩

Kakunen mushō kore ikan.   Tesshū kōho

**Whatever is this – 'Vast emptiness, nothing sacred!
Tesshū kōho.**

This comes from the episode when the
Emperor of China asked Bodhidharma,
the Great Patriach of Zen, 'What
is the first principle of Buddhism?'
Bodhidharma replied, 'Vast emptiness,
nothing sacred!' (From the *Blue Cliff
Record*, a *kōan* collection compiled
in the eleventh century by Xue Tou).
Bodhidharma (Daruma in Japanese) is
represented here as a snowman, whose
lack of a stable shape can be likened to
the formlessness of the Buddha-nature.

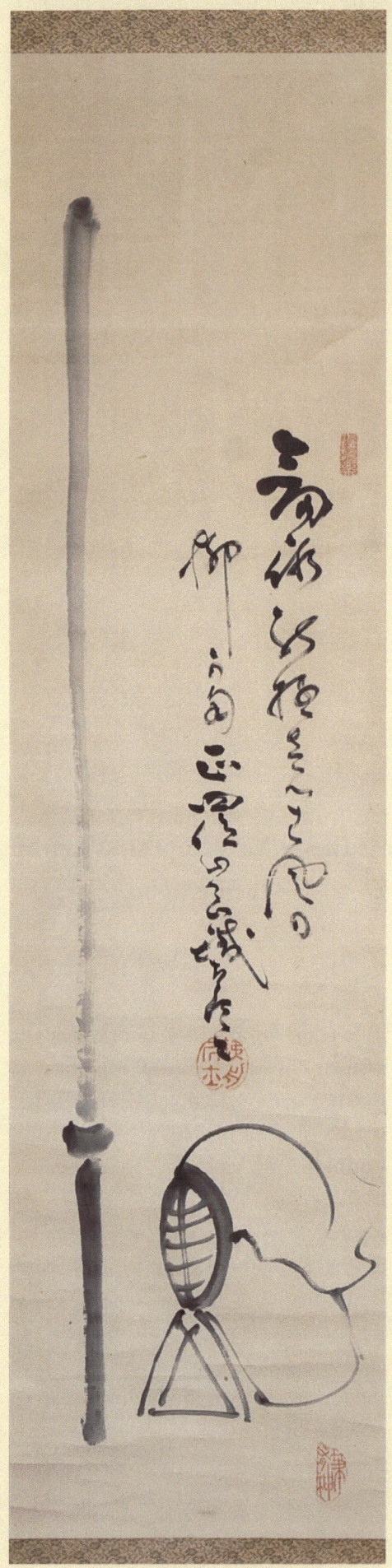

Yamaoka Tesshū (1836–1888)

Kendō helmet and bamboo sword (with inscription in cursive script) 1886. *Sumi* ink on paper 130cm × 30cm.

剣術の極意は風の柳かな

正四位山岡鐵太郎書

Kenjutsu no gokui wa kaze no yanagi kana　　*Shōshii Yamaoka Tetsutarō sho*

The mystique of fencing is like the willows in the wind. Yamaoka Tetsutarō, Senior Fourth Court Rank.

Tesshū is said to have studied *kendō*, Zen and calligraphy even when he was suffering from cancer in the last years of his life. His determination to live life to the full resonates powerfully in this work.

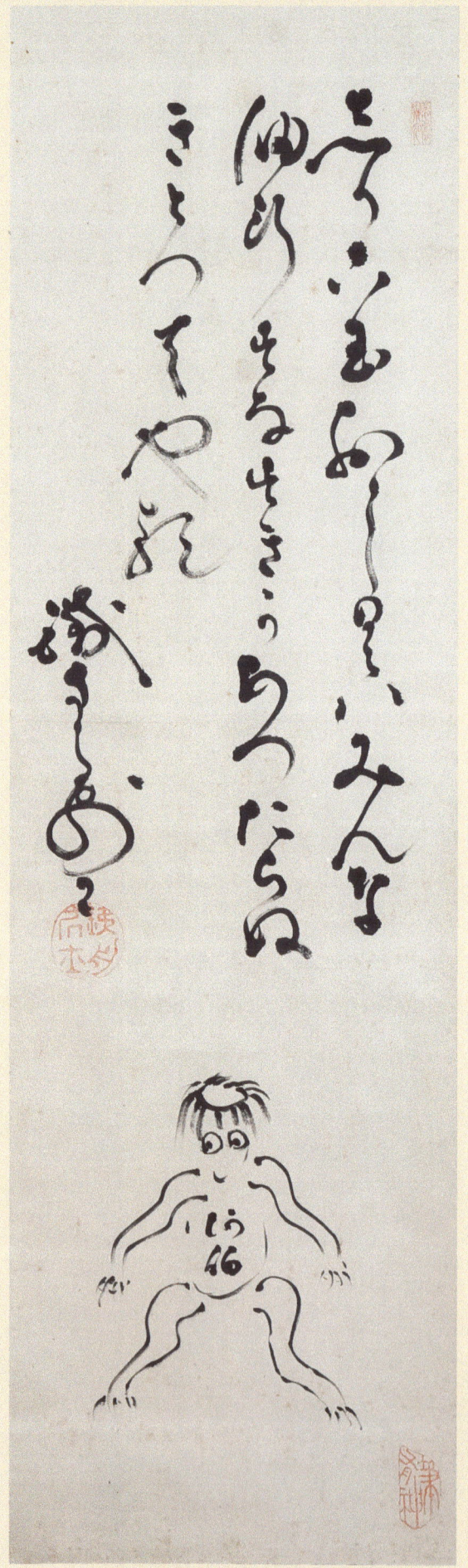

Yamaoka Tesshū (1836–1888)
Kappa (with inscription in cursive script) 1886. *Sumi* ink on paper 98cm × 29cm.

しりこ玉　おしくばみんな
油断すな　すきがあったら
ぬきとってやる

鉄舟高歩書

Shirikodama Oshikuba minna Yudan suna Suki ga attara Nukitotte yaru　　*Tesshū kōho sho*

**Don't hesitate, trying to protect your backside as soon a hole appears - seize it!
Written by Tesshū kōho.**

Kappa are fantastic water sprites, whose attributes include being formidable wrestlers of great fighting spirit who like to tear out their opponents' livers through their anuses.

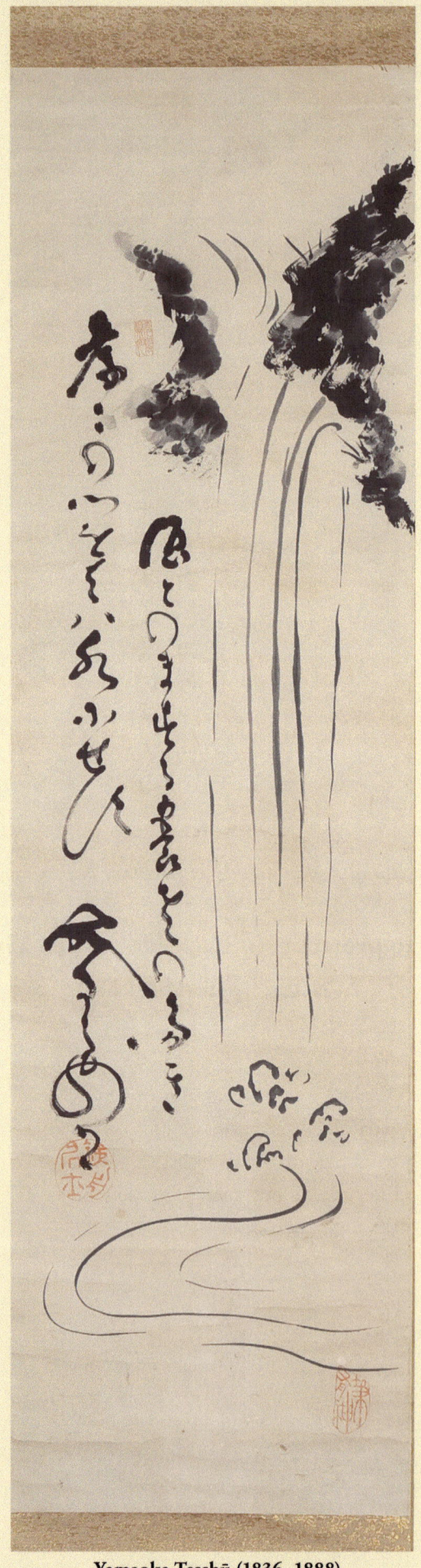

Yamaoka Tesshū (1836–1888)
Waterfall (with inscription in cursive script) 1888. *Sumi* ink on paper 109cm × 30cm.

孝々の心を天は水にせず
酒とのまする養老のたき
鉄舟高歩書

Kōkō no Kokoro o ten wa Mizu ni sezu Sake to nomasuru Yōrō no taki   Tesshū kōho sho

**Be filial to your aged parents - instead of water,
heaven will provide them with a gentle waterfall of *sake*.
Written by Tesshū kōho.**

This rendering of a waterfall accompanied by an inscription based on a Chinese poem was brushed by Tesshū in the last year of his life. For many years he had studied the calligraphic styles of the Chinese master Wang Xizhi (303-361) and the Japanese monk Kōbō Daishi (774-835, also known as Kūkai).

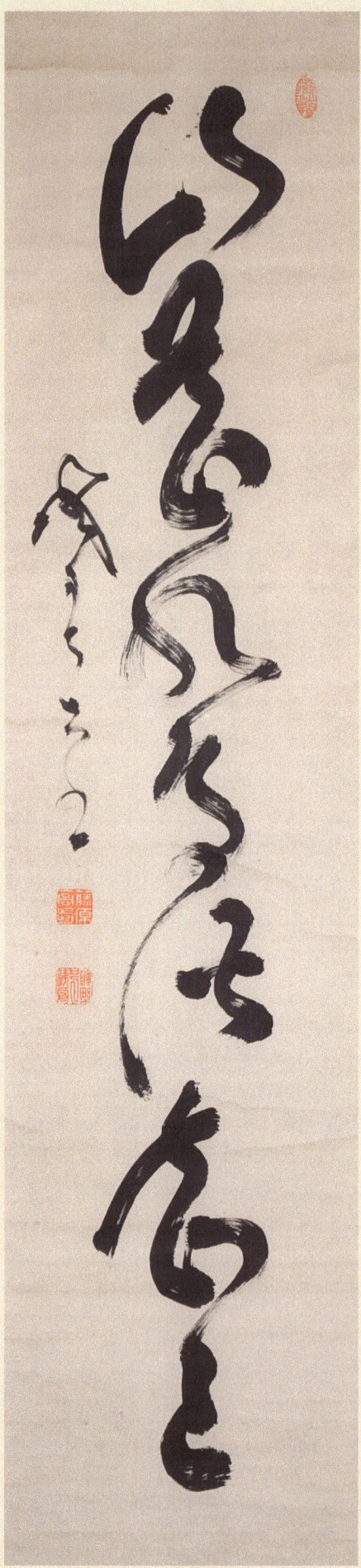

Yamaoka Tesshū (1836–1888)
One line saying (cursive script) 1887. *Sumi* ink on paper 130cm × 30cm.

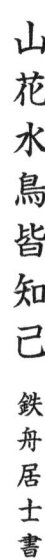

山花水鳥皆知己　鉄舟居士書

Sanka suichō mina chiki　Tesshū koji sho

**The mountains, flowers, water and birds are all good friends of mine.
Written by Tesshū koji.**

Like the subject alluded to, the rhythm and flow of this single column of brushed characters are harmonious. Tesshū developed a distinctly personal style, cultivating calligraphy through the *ki-ai* of swordsmanship and the principles of Zen.

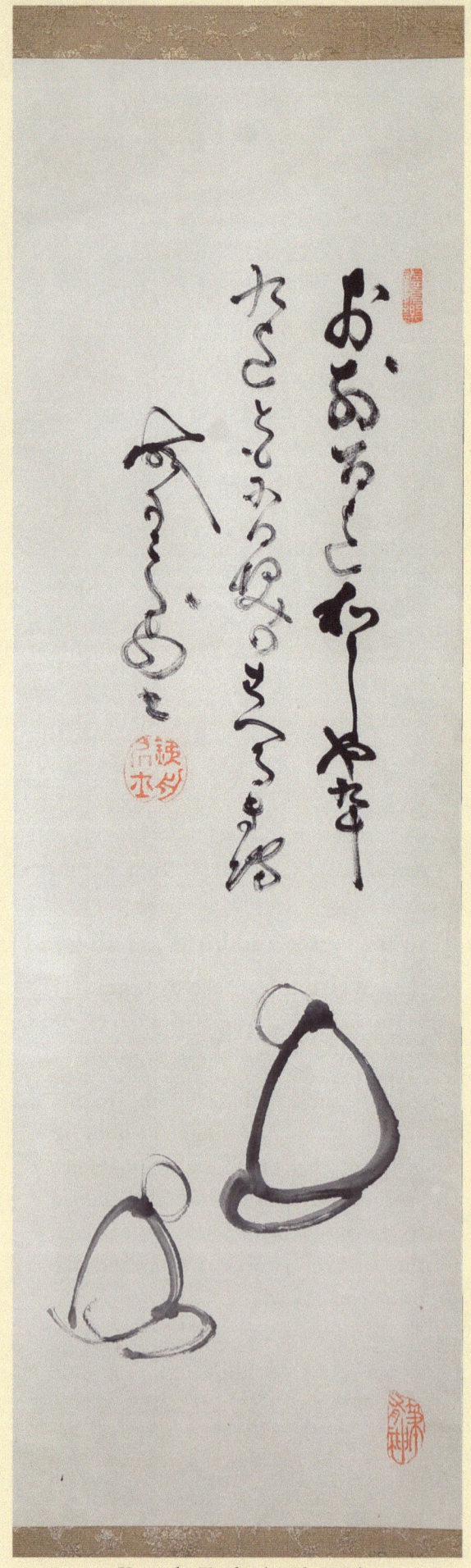

Yamaoka Tesshū (1836–1888)
Two figures (with inscription in cursive script) 1885. *Sumi* ink on paper 103cm × 31cm.

お前百迄わしや九十九迄
ともに白髪のはえるまで

鉄舟高歩書

Omae hyaku made washa kujyūku made tomo ni shiraga no haeru made   Tesshū kōho sho

As you reach one hundred and I reach ninety-nine,
our hair will turn white together.
Written by Tesshū kōho.

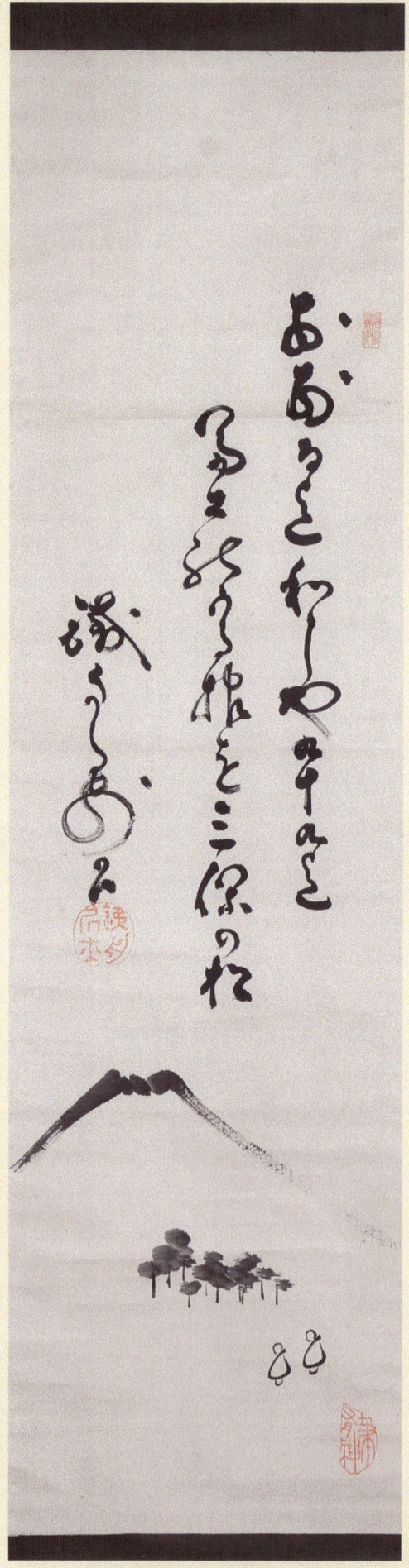

Yamaoka Tesshū (1836–1888)
Mount Fuji, pines and two figures (with inscription in cursive script) 1887-8. *Sumi* ink on paper 109cm × 29cm.

お前百迄わしや九十九迄
富士の高ねを三保の松
鉄舟高歩書

Omae hyaku made washa kujyūku made Fuji no takane o miho no matsu   Tesshū kōho sho

**You'll reach one hundred as I become ninety-nine
the peak of Mount Fuji and the pines of Miho.
Written by Tesshū kōho.**

The practice of inscribing poetry in the blank space of a painting was established by Chinese scholar-painters during the Song dynasty (960-1279). The inscription usually expresses what the painting alone cannot. In this case the vastness of nature in terms of time and space are alluded to.

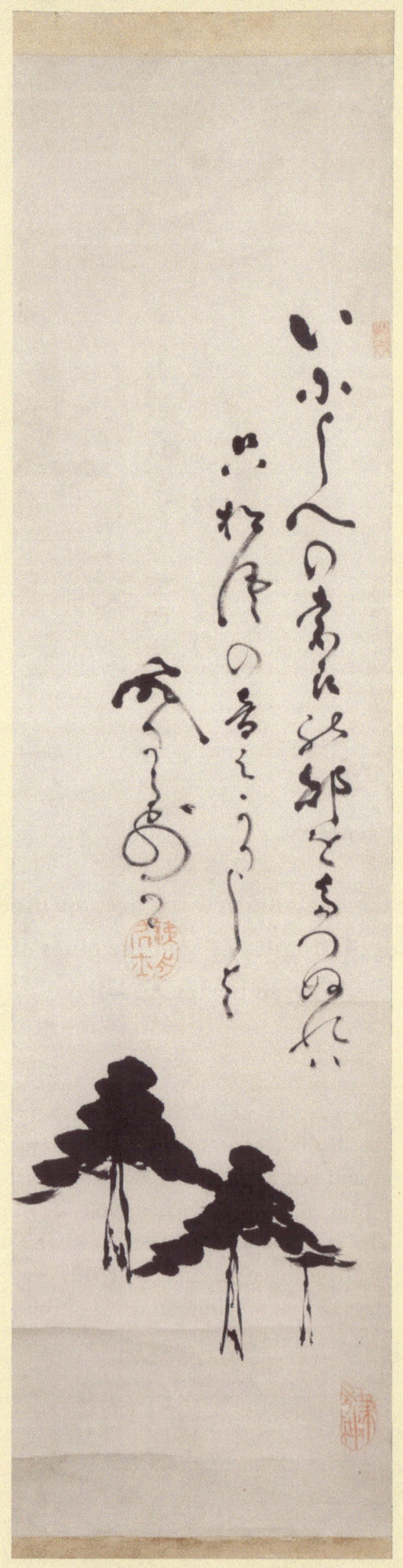

Yamaoka Tesshū (1836–1888)
Three pines (with inscription in cursive script) 1888. *Sumi* ink on paper 110cm × 28cm.

いにしへの奈良の都をたづぬれば
只松風の音ばかりして

鉄舟高歩書

Inishie no Nara no miyako o Tazunureba Tada matsukaze no Oto bakari shite   Tesshū kōho sho

A visit to the ancient capital of Nara
all that remains is the sound of the wind blowing through the pines.
Written by Tesshū kōho.

The ancient city of Heijō-kyō, now known as Nara, was established in 710. It was the capital of Japan until 794, when the emperor moved to Kyoto. The artistic standards achieved during this period are generally considered to mark the height of Buddhist culture in Japan. A pure breeze rustling through the pines blocks out the dust of this world. In ancient Japanese and Chinese texts, 'dust' refers to the constraints of the everyday world.

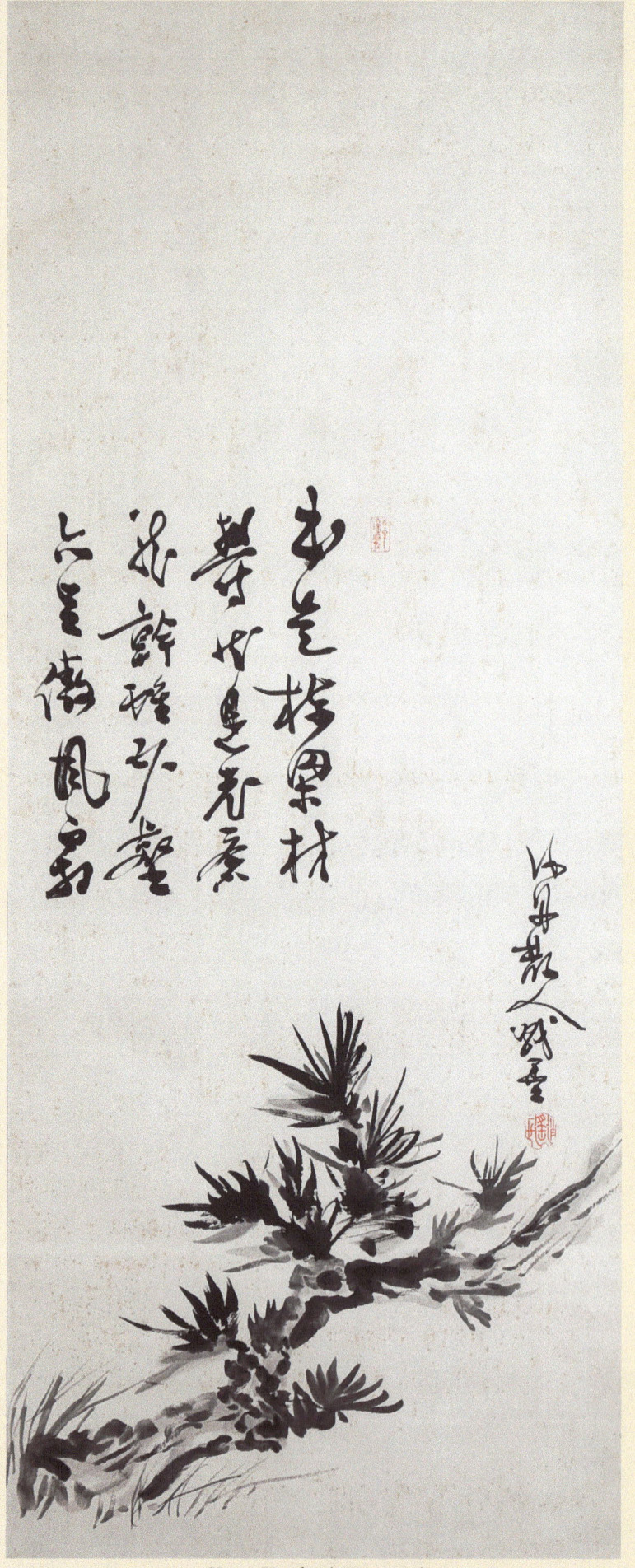

Katsu Kaishū (1823-1899)
Pine (with inscription in cursive script) 1895. *Sumi* ink on paper 134cm × 53cm.

本是れ棟梁の材
鬱然として老蒼を見る
龍幹壑に臥すと雖も
亦風霜に傲るに足る
海舟散人戯

Moto kore tōryō no zai utsuzen to shite rōsō o miru ryū kan tani ni gasu to iedomo mata fūsō ni ogoru ni taru   Kaishū sanjingi

True this pillar of wood, which resembles a dragon, its trunk prostrating, nevertheless able to withstand the hardships of wind and frost. The dissipated fool, Kaishū.

Katsu Kaishū was born in Edo (modern day Tokyo) to a samurai family serving the Tokugawa shogun. From his childhood he learned swordsmanship from the famous teacher Otani Nobutomo. Kaishū also studied Zen at Ushijima Kōfukuji Temple in Tokyo. Later he became interested in Dutch and Western martial studies. He was one of Japan's earliest internationalists and in 1860 commanded the ship that carried Japan's first delegation to the United States. Kaishū played a central role, along with Tesshū, in the transfer of power from the Tokugawa shogunate to the Meiji Emperor. Kaishū was well versed in the Chinese classics, calligraphy, poetry and the martial arts.

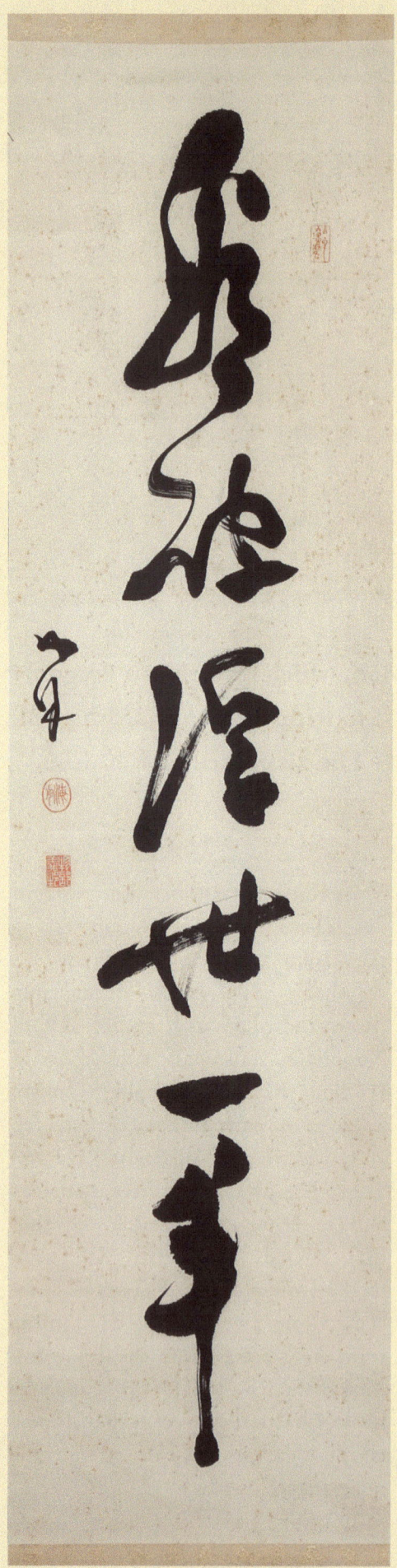

Katsu Kaishū (1823-1899)
One line saying (Cursive script) 1895. *Sumi* ink on paper 115cm × 31cm.

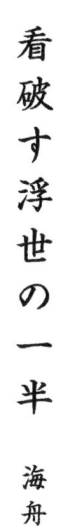

看破す浮世の一半　海舟

Kanpasu ukiyo no ippan　Kaishū

See into the transient world and penetrate through it. Kaishū.

Kaishū felt that the principles of swordsmanship and the conducting of foreign affairs were the same, namely to keep the mind clear and serene like a bright mirror and not to allow illusions or misconceptions to cloud the matter at hand. This work is considered an outstanding example of the single-column calligraphy of Kaishū's later years, the first two characters being especially refined.

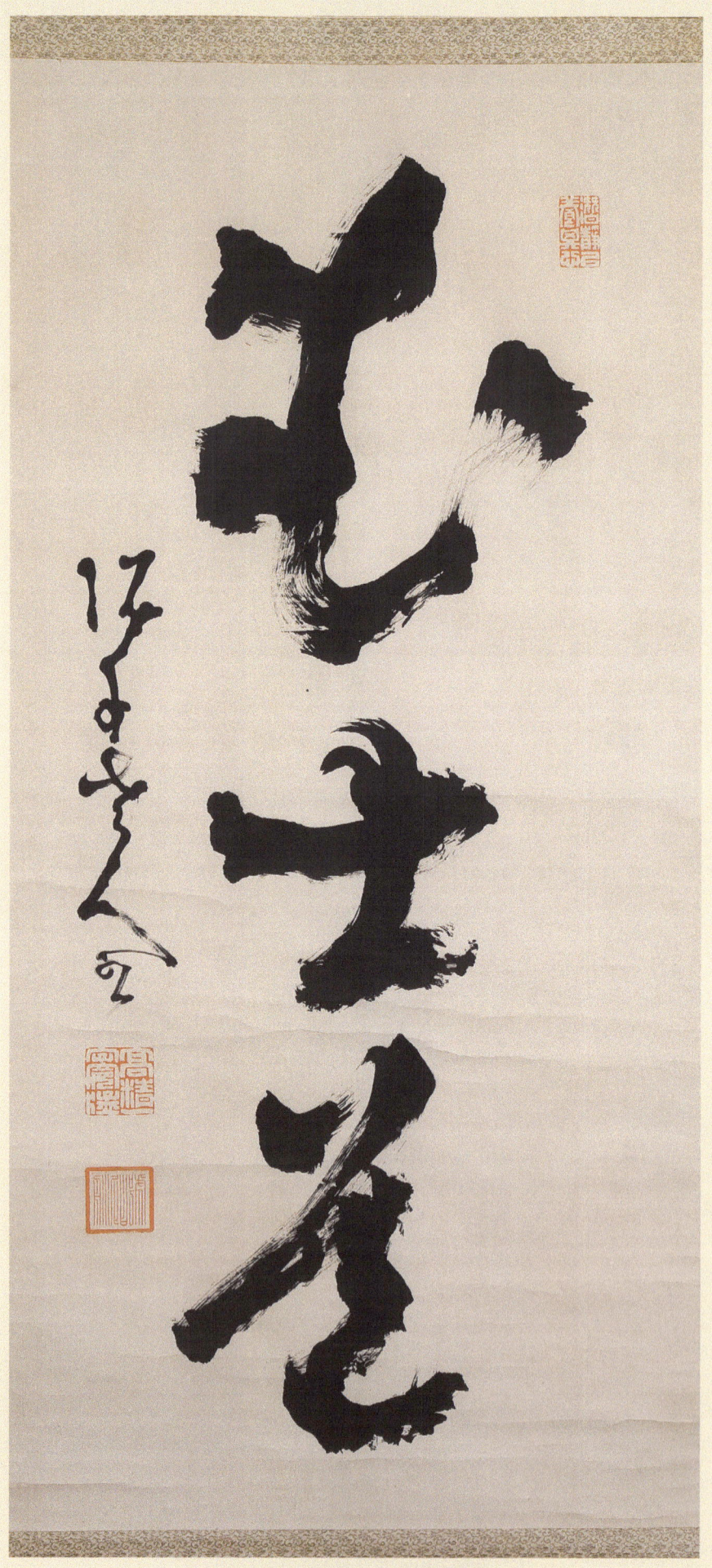

Takahashi Deishū (1835–1903)
One line saying (cursive script) 1900. *Sumi* ink on paper 134cm × 64cm.

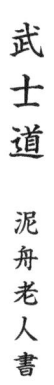

武士道　泥舟老人書

Bushidō　Deishū rōjin sho

The Way of the Warrior.
Written by the old man Deishū.

Takahashi Deishū was an expert in spear fighting who served as a minister in the district of Ise, and was an important figure in the last days of the Tokugawa government. He retired from public life soon after the Meiji Restoration of 1868 to devote himself to poetry, calligraphy and painting. During the time he was studying calligraphy under Nagatani Kawakane he stated, "In extending the brush head instead of the spear, one must reveal the truth of enlightenment." Deishū created this calligraphy at the age of sixty-five.

蚯蚓内無筋骨之強外無爪牙之利

然下飲黄泉上墾乾土何用心一也

人能一志事無不成

為長谷川氏　泥舟精

Takahashi Deishū (1835–1903)
Three line saying (regular script) 1885. *Sumi* ink on silk 116cm × 33cm.

蚯蚓は内に筋骨の強無く
外に爪牙の利無し
然れども下は黄泉を飲み
上は乾土を墾やすは何ん心を
用いること一なれば也
人能志を一にすれば
事成らざる無し

長谷川氏の為　泥舟精

Mimizu wa uchi ni kinkotsu no kyō naku soto ni sōga no ri nashi
shikaredomo shita wa kōsen o nomi Ue wa kendo o tagayasu wa ikan kokoro o mochiiru koto itsu nareba nari
Hito yoku kokorozashi o itsu ni sureba koto narazaru nashi
Hasegawa shi no tame　Deishū sei

The earthworm cannot take advantage of the might of sinews and bones or nails
and fangs as it is lacking in all of these.
So what is it that enables it to drink from the sweet spring far beneath the earth
and to cultivate the dry soil on the surface of the earth?
It is because of the earthworm's spirit.
If a true man unifies ability and mind, then there will be nothing he cannot accomplish.
Written at the request of Mr Hasegawa, Deishū's spirit.

'*Dei-shū*' literally translates as 'mud-boat'. Deishū adopted this name at the age of 37, thereafter contenting himself with a life of refined poverty, supported by his brother-in-law Yamaoka Tesshū.

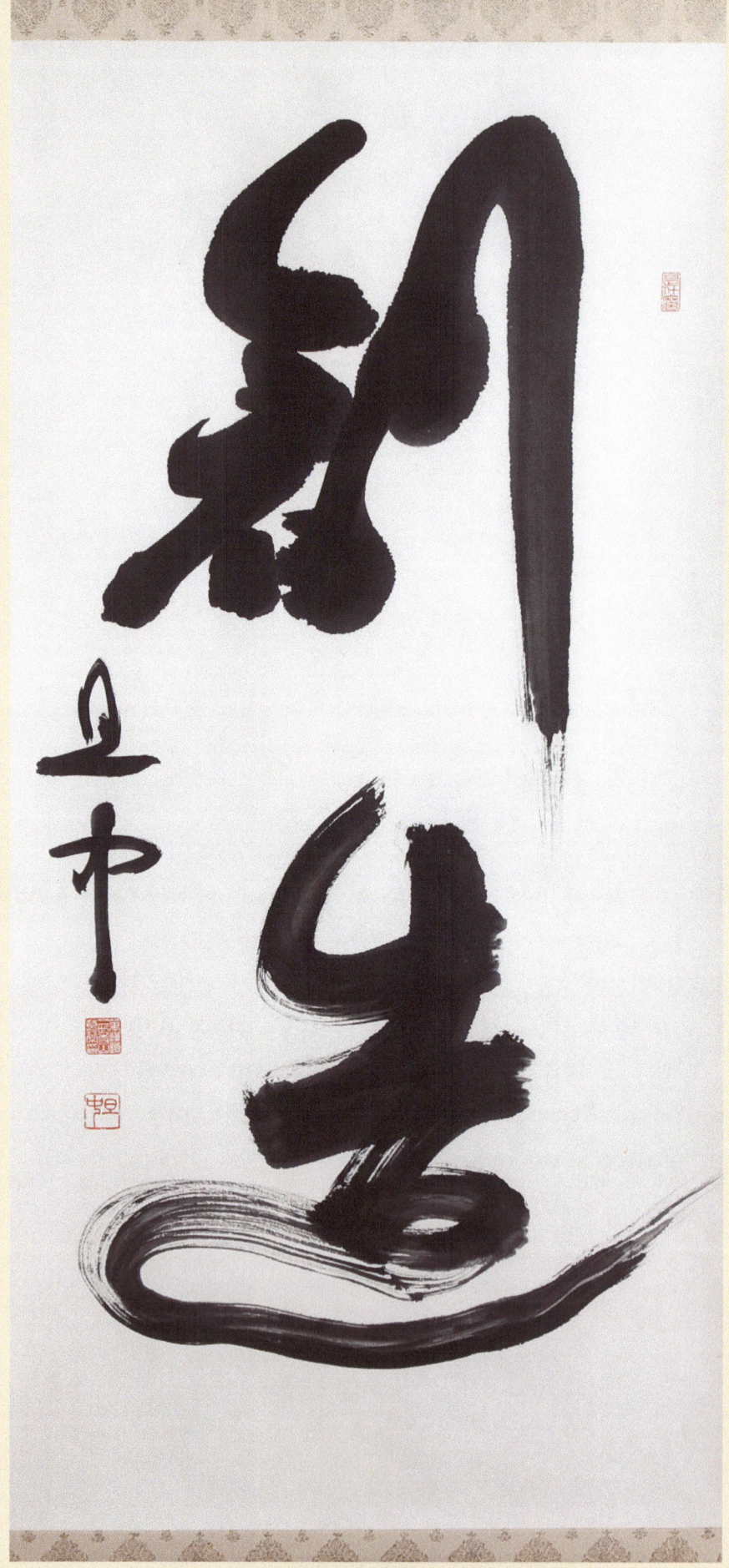

Terayama Tanchū (1938–2007)
One line saying (cursive script) Autumn 2004. *Sumi* ink on paper 164cm × 33cm.

創
造

旦
中

Sōzō   Tanchū

Creation.
Tanchū.

旦 or *tan* means dawn, 中 or *chū* means
middle or centre. Zen calligraphers
often sign with their *inka* pen names
(name given by a master to a disciple on
recognition of a significant realisation).
The twentieth century Rinzai Zen
master Ōmori Sōgen Rōshi gave this
name to his disciple Terayama Katsujō
at the age of 36. This name – 'in the
centre of the dawn' in Zen terms also
suggests an awakening or dawning.

Courtesy of St. Hugh's College, Oxford

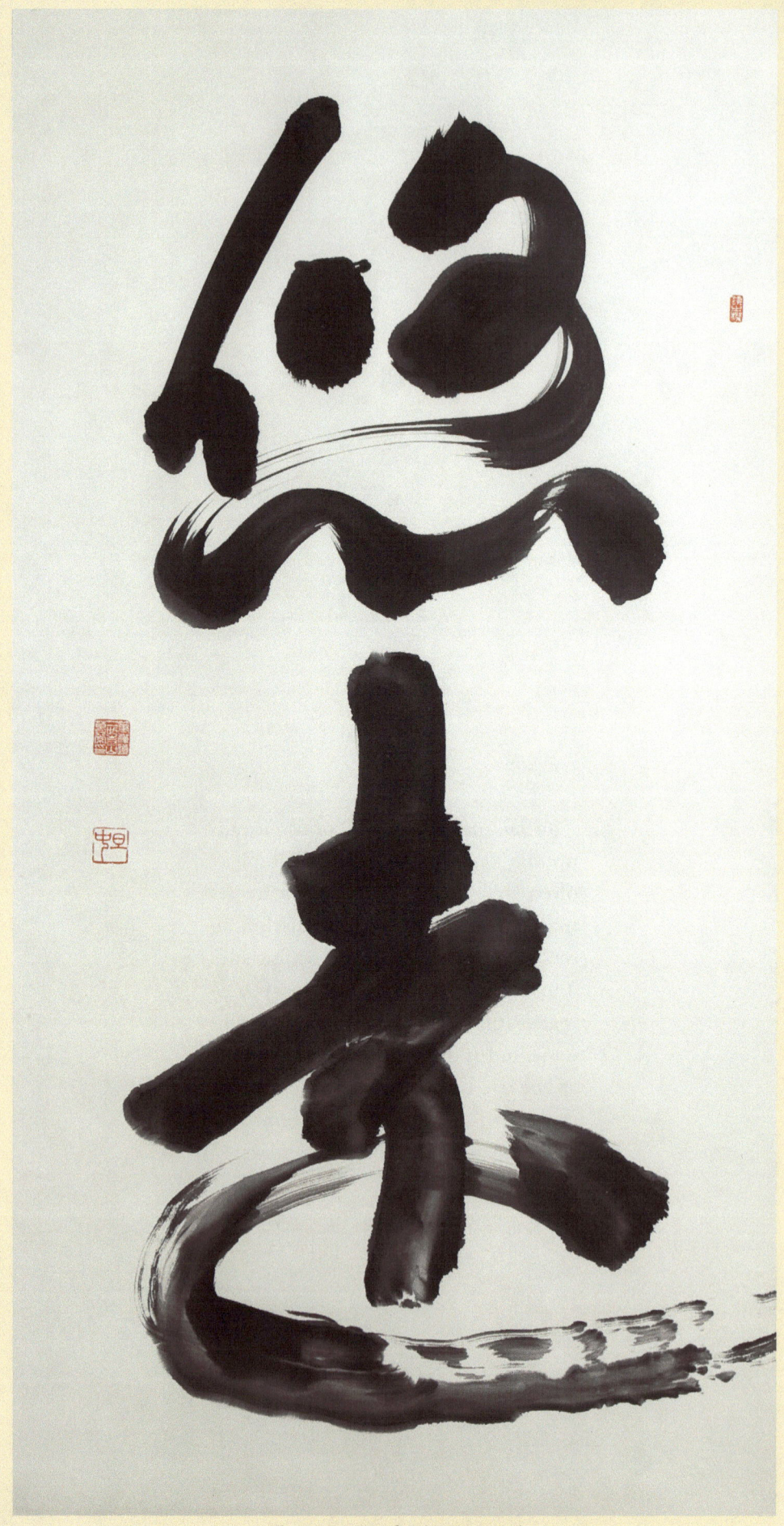

Terayama Tanchū (1938–2007)
One line saying (cursive script) autumn 2006. *Sumi* ink on paper 136cm × 64cm.

Yūen

Infinite space.

In this calligraphy the name 'Tanchū' is represented in the seal impression which is the final touch in creating a calligraphy.

Courtesy of the Victoria and Albert Museum

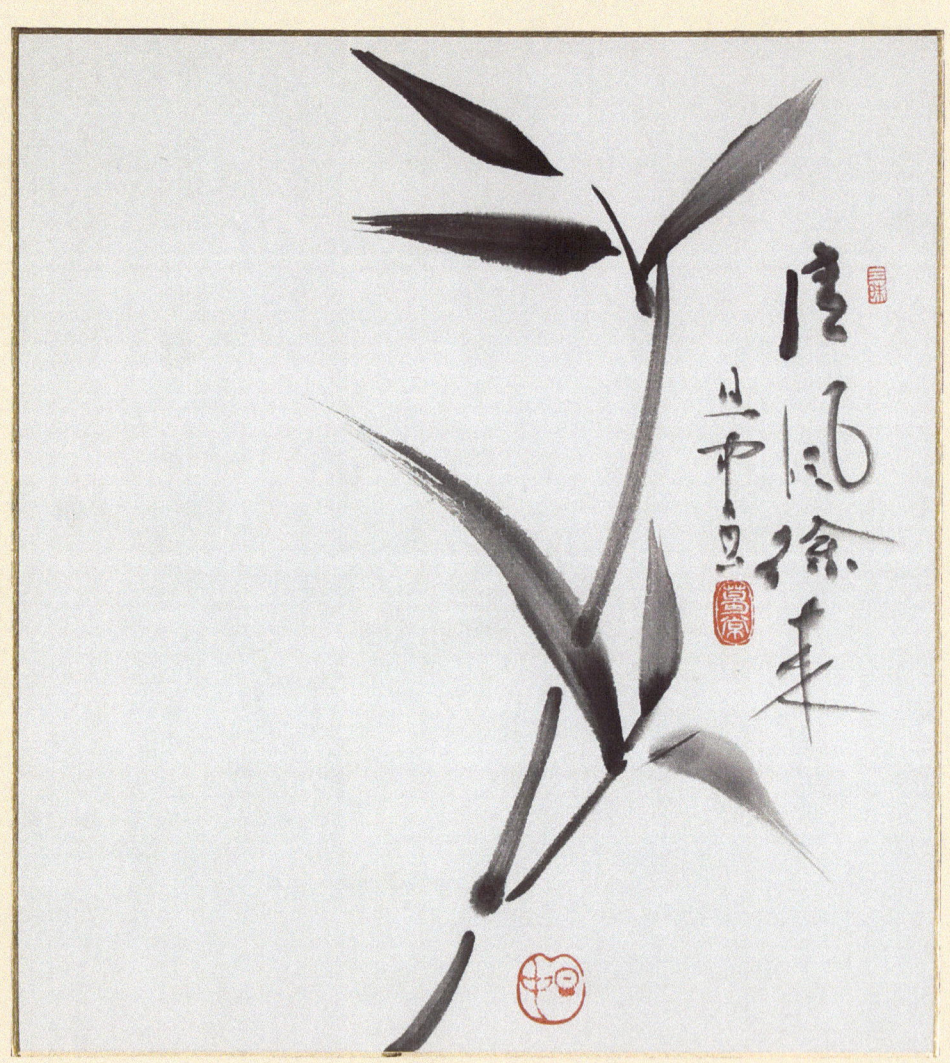

Terayama Tanchū (1938–2007)
Bamboo (with inscription in cursive script) 2006. *Sumi* ink on poem card 17cm × 16cm.

清風徐来

旦中書

Seifū jorai   Tanchū sho

The fresh wind comes softly. Written by Tanchū.

According to Chinese tradition, painting and calligraphy are one and the same. Orchid, bamboo, plum blossom and chrysanthemum were known as the 'Four Gentlemen'. Bamboo, like pine, is evergreen and survives the cold of winter and the heat of the summer, the intensities of which may be understood as a metaphor for the human condition.

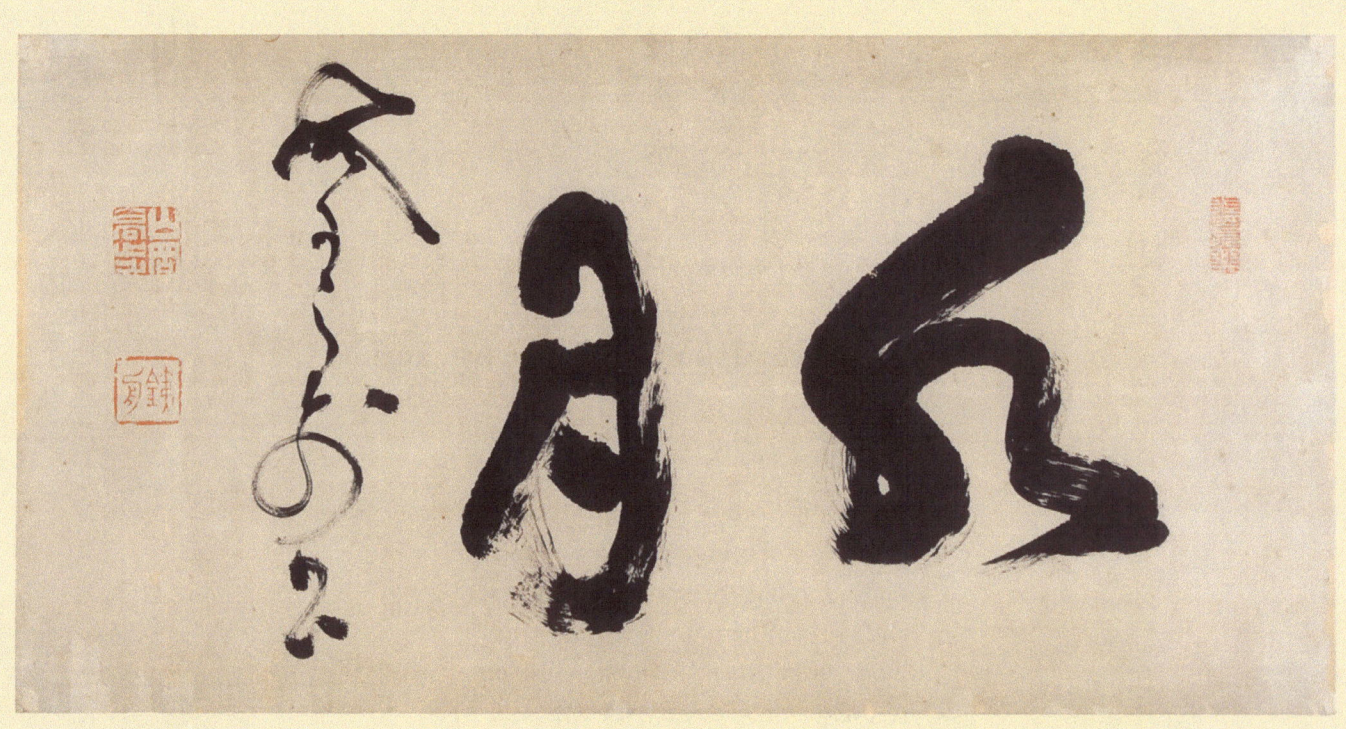

Yamaoka Tesshū (1836–1888)
Water-moon (cursive script) 1888? *Sumi* ink on paper 33cm × 68cm.

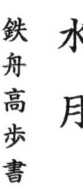

Suigetsu   Tesshū kōho sho

Water-moon.

Written by Tesshū kōho.

'Water-moon' is an important concept in both swordsmanship and Zen. The ideal state of mind is symbolised by the moon naturally reflecting in water, in perfect accord. Water receives the moonlight without discrimination and the moon illuminates all things without discrimination. Both characters project strength and stability and are extremely well formed. Tesshū's signature balances the character for moon which has been written slightly lower than the character for water.

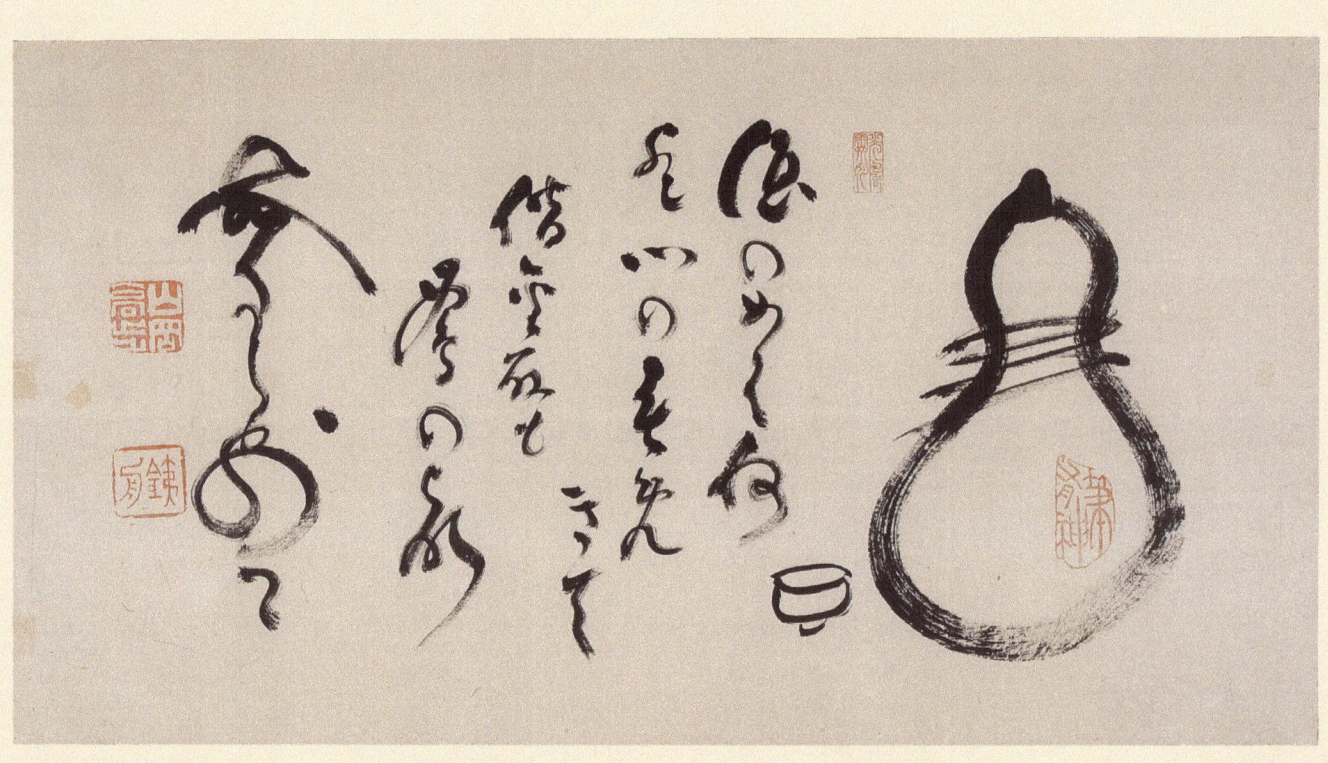

Yamaoka Tesshū (1836–1888)
Sake gourd and cup (with inscription in cursive script) 1886? *Sumi* ink on paper 31.5cm × 57cm.

酒のめ者
何登心の春免き天
借金取も鶯の聲
鉄舟高歩書

Sake nomeba nanto kokoro no haru meki te shakkin torimo uguisu no koe.   *Tesshū kōho sho*

When you drink *sake* you feel spring in your heart.
Even the debt collector sounds like the nightingale's song.
Written by Tesshū kōho.

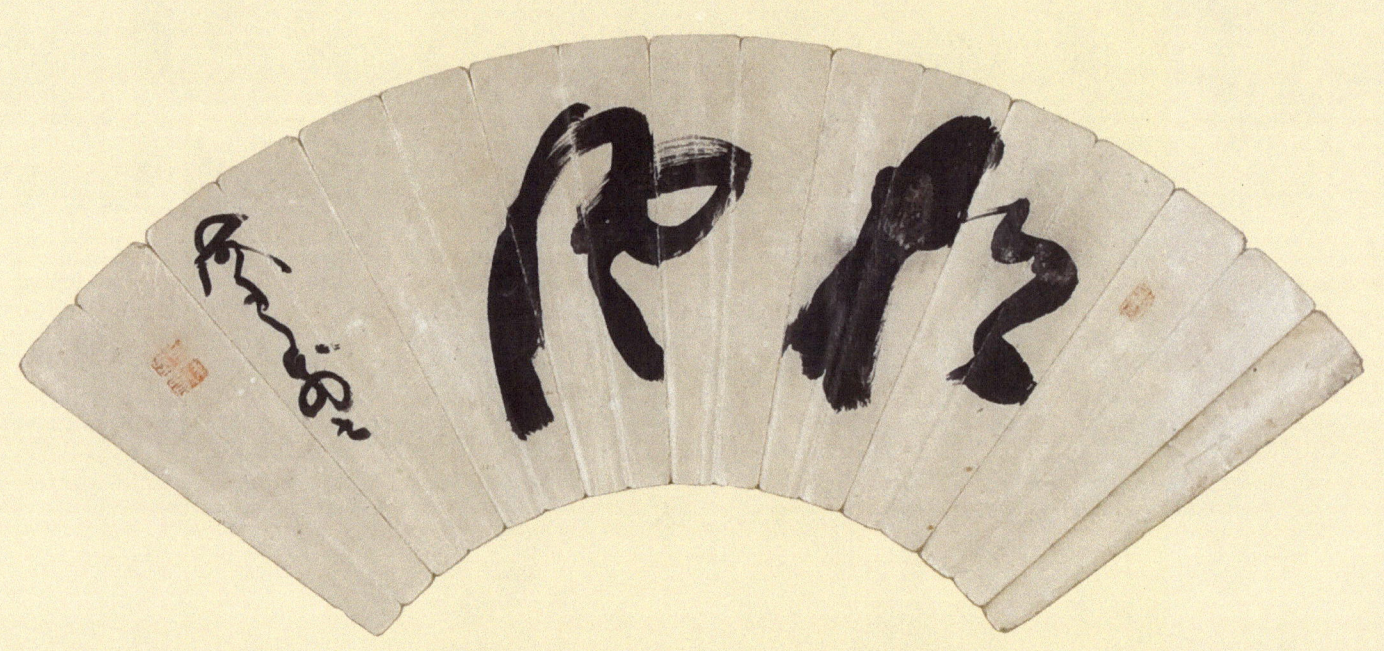

Yamaoka Tesshū (1836–1888)
Pine wind. 1887? *Sumi* ink on fan (mounted) 15cm × 42cm.

松
風

鉄舟高歩書

Shōfū.   Tesshū kōho sho

Pine Wind.
Written by Tesshū kōho.

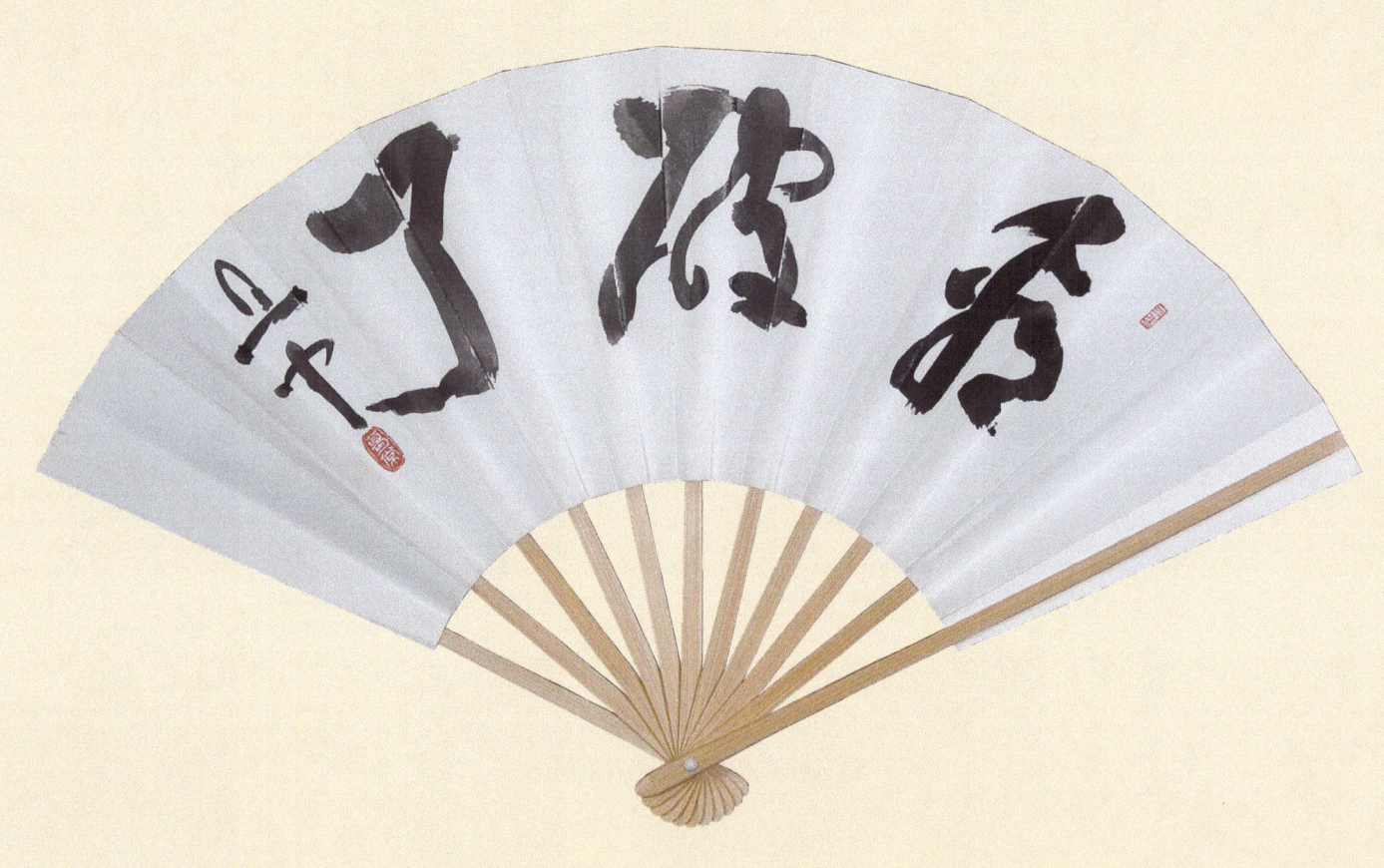

Terayama Tanchū (1938–2007)
Kanpa ryō. 2006. *Sumi* ink on fan. 15cm × 42cm.

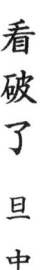

Kanpa ryō. Tanchū

**Seeing through and through.
Tanchū.**

The first two characters of this calligraphy are the same as the *kanpa* (first two characters) of the calligraphy written by Katsu Kaishū on page 63. Terayama Tanchū thought highly of this calligraphy by Kaishū.

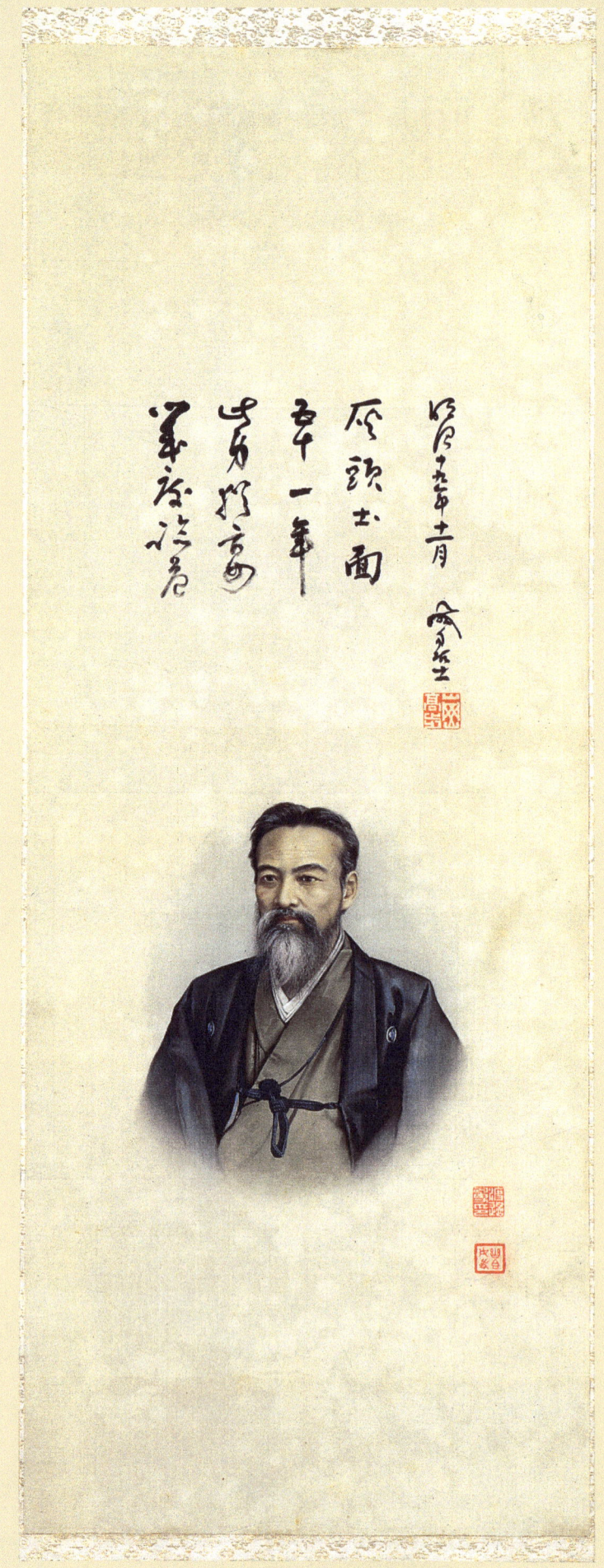

Yamaoka Tesshū (1836–1888)
Portrait (with inscription in cursive script) 1886. *Sumi* ink on paper. Zenshōan collection.

灰頭土面
五十一年
此身猶薗
幾度臨危

明治十九年十一月　鉄舟居士

Ikudo kini nozomi konomi nao o tonoshimu gojūichi nen haitodomen
Meiji Jūku nen jūichi gatsu　Tesshū koji

How many times was my life in danger?
Now I enjoy a continuous banquet.
Fifty-one years – a dusty head and a dirty face.
Tesshū koji.

This is a formal portrait of Tesshū made when he was 51. The inscription is by Tesshū, it reads from top left to bottom right.

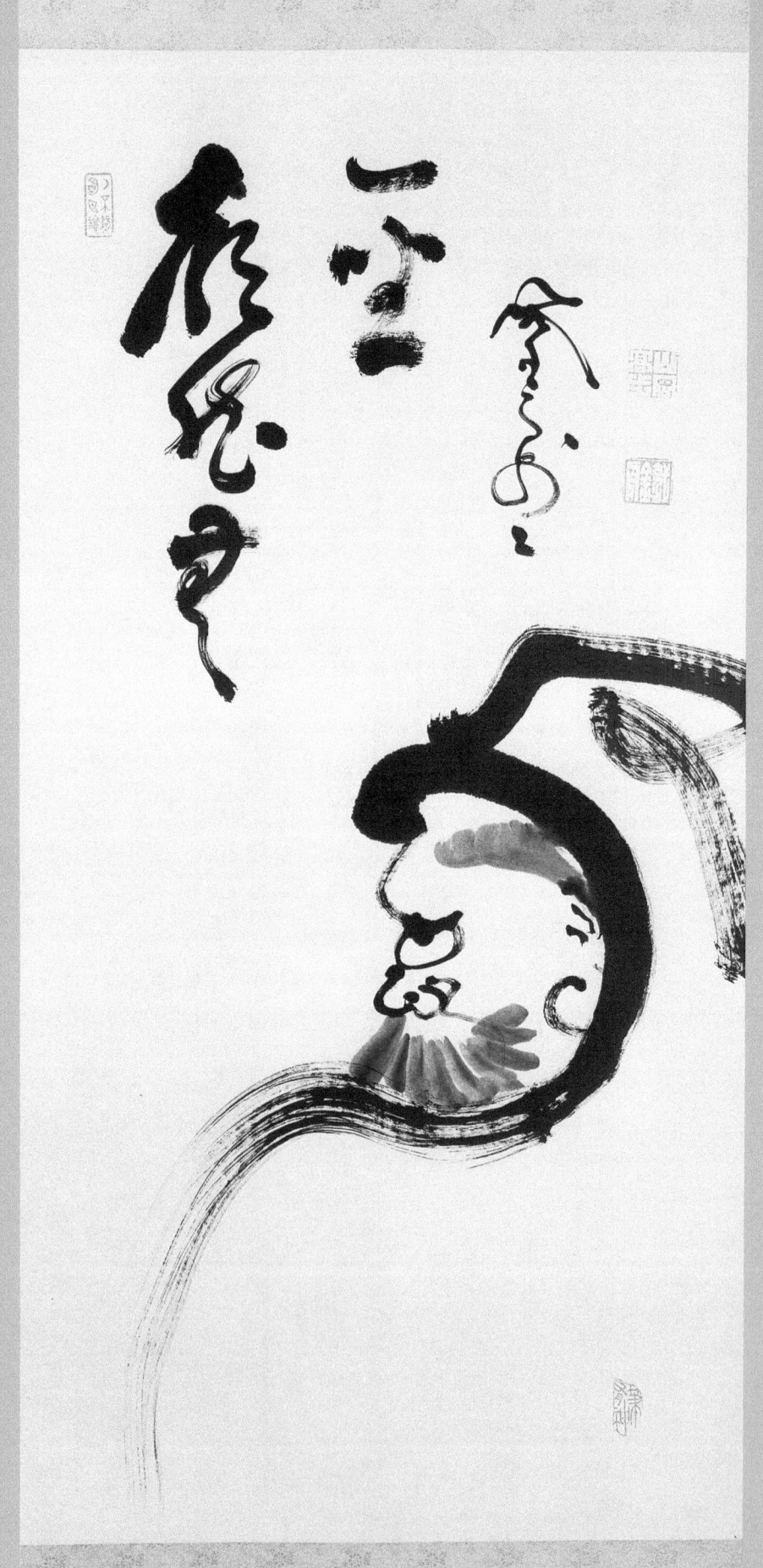

Yamaoka Tesshū (1836–1888)
Portrait of Bodhidharma (with inscription in cursive script). *Sumi* ink on paper. Zenshōan collection.

廓
然
無
聖

鉄
舟
高
歩

Kakunen mushō. Tesshū kōho.

Vast emptiness – nothing sacred!
Tesshū kōho.

Drawn in profile, this Daruma has
been brushed deftly, in a few strokes.
The abbreviated inscription in cursive
script reads from left to right. The head
of the Bodhidharma is placed facing
to the left of the composition, and
Tesshū's signature and seal impression
are placed to the right and slightly
behind Bodhidharma's head as a sign
of deference.

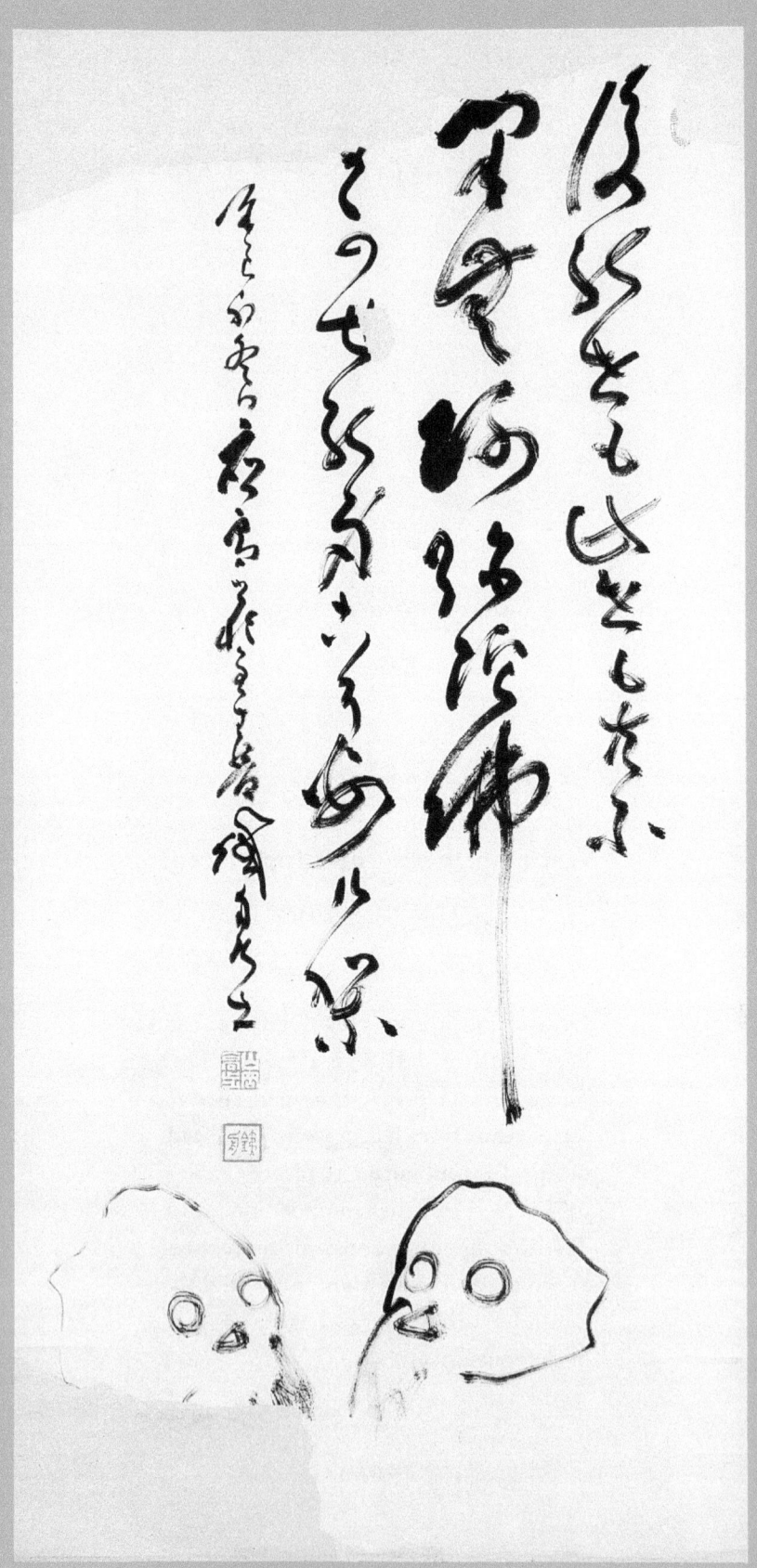

Yamaoka Tesshū (1836–1888)
Namu Amida Butsu (painting of two skulls with inscription in cursive script). *Sumi* ink on paper. Zenshōan collection.

南
無
阿
弥
陀
仏

Namu Amida Butsu.   Tesshū koji.

Hail! To Amida Buddha
Written by Tesshū koji.

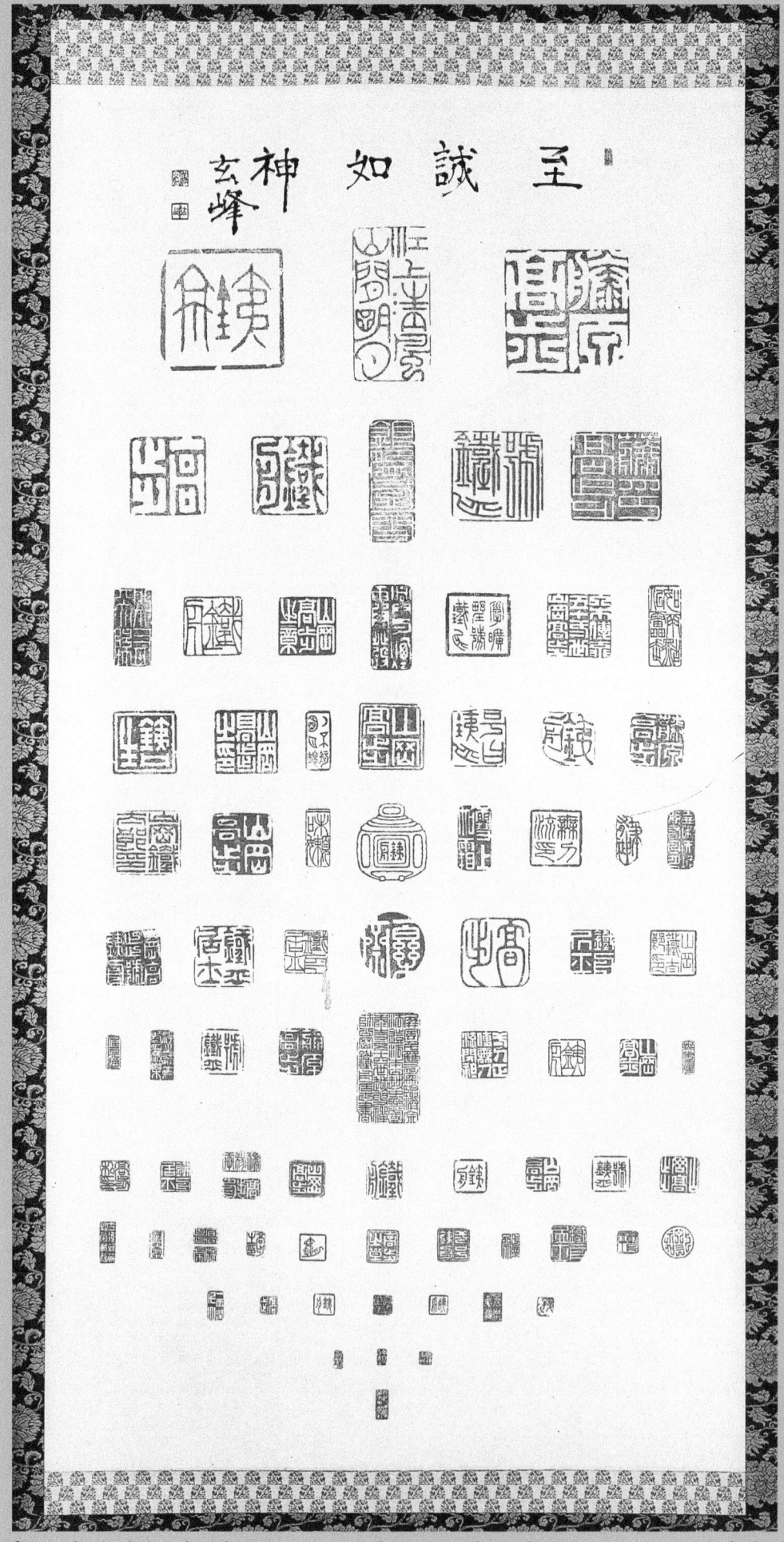

Record of Yamaoka Tesshū's seals with inscription in regular script at the top by Yamamoto Gempō Rōshi (1866-1961). Seal impressions on paper and *sumi* ink. Zenshōan collection.

至
誠
如
神

玄
峰

Makoto wa kami ni itaru gotoshi. Gempō.

Sincerity is god-like.
Gempō.

This is a record of 79 seal impressions from Tesshū's seals. Yamamoto Gempō Rōshi was a well known Zen teacher of the twentieth century. He was the abbot of Myōshinji Temple in Kyoto for a brief period. Gempō Rōshi also lived at Zenshōan for a short time.

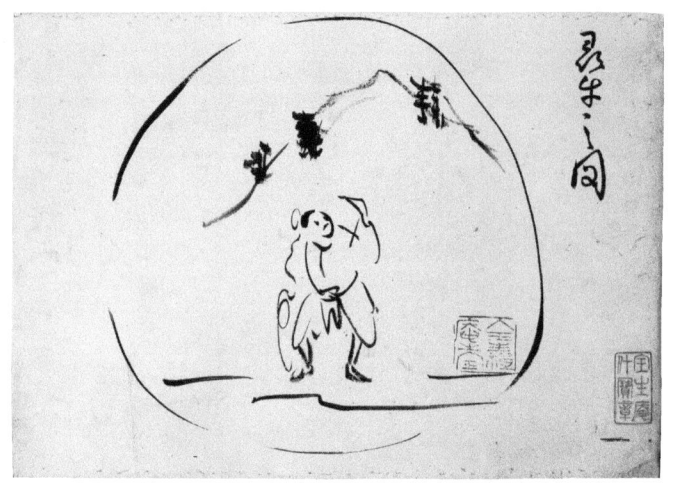

十牛図第一　尋牛之図

① Looking for the ox

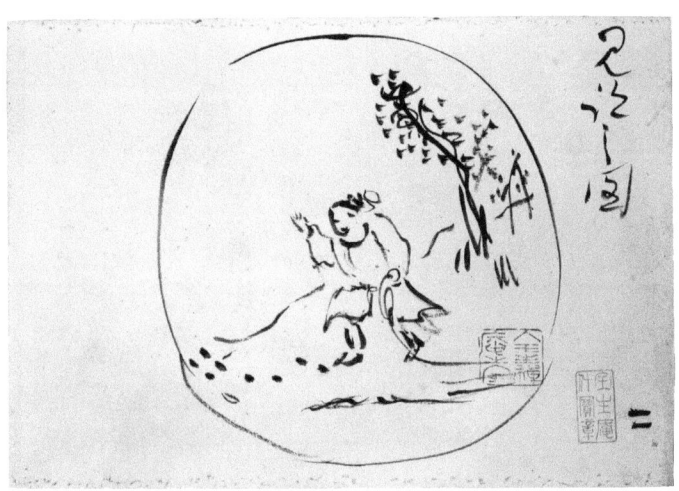

十牛図第二　見跡之図

② Seeing the traces of the ox

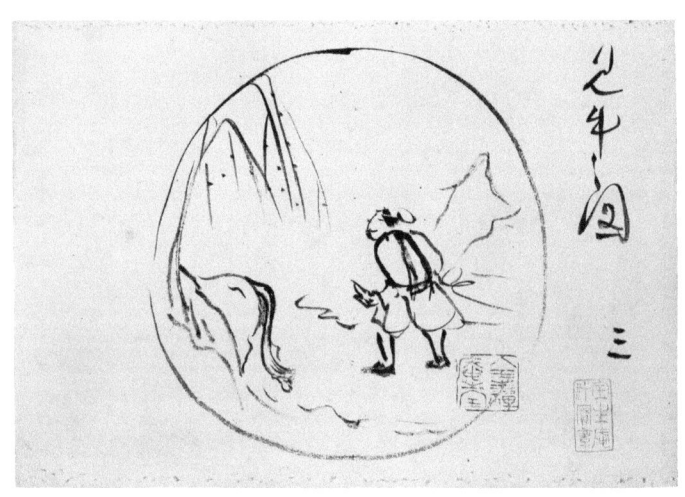

十牛図第三　見牛之図

③ Seeing the ox

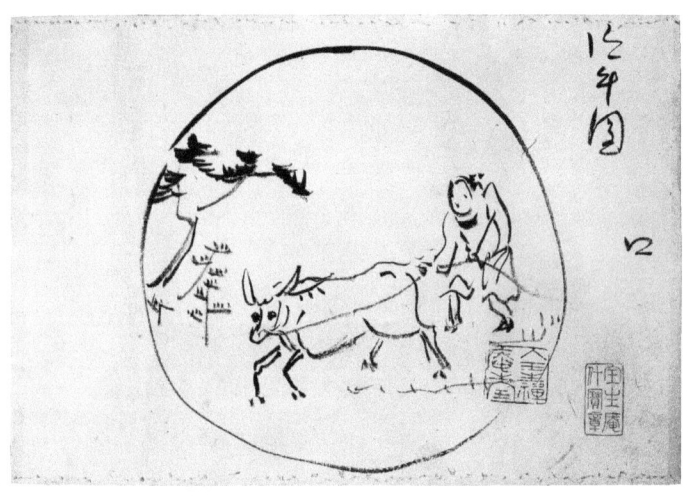

十牛図第四　得牛之図

④ Catching the ox

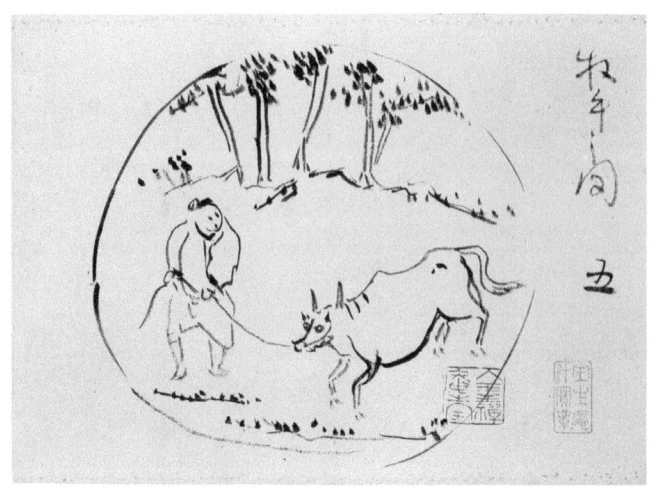

十牛図第五　牧牛之図

⑤ Herding the ox

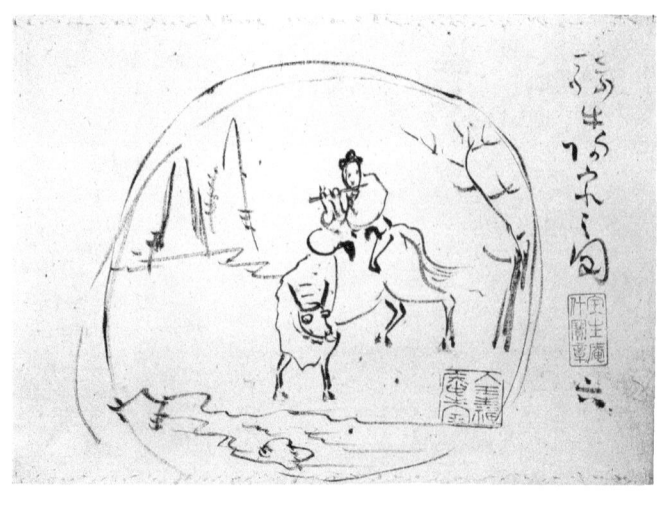

十牛図第六　騎牛家之図

⑥ Coming home on the ox's back

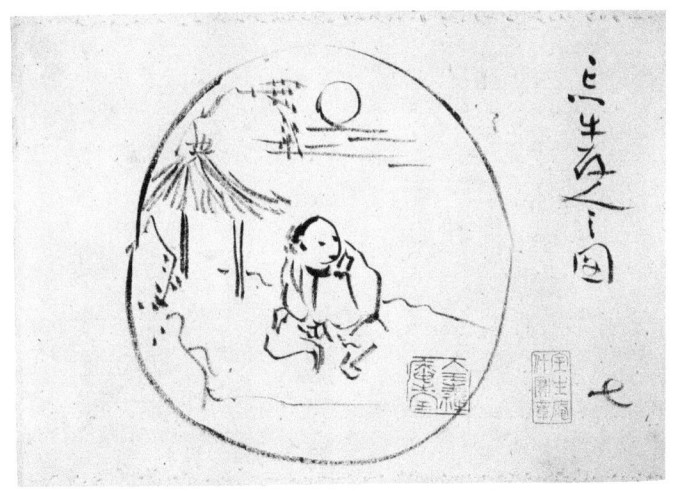

十牛図第七　忘牛存人之図

⑦ The ox forgotten, leaving the man alone

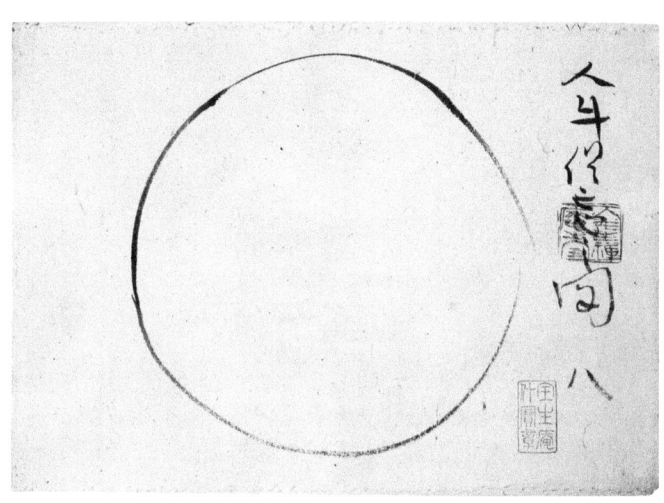

十牛図第八　人牛俱忘之図

⑧ The ox and the man both gone out of sight

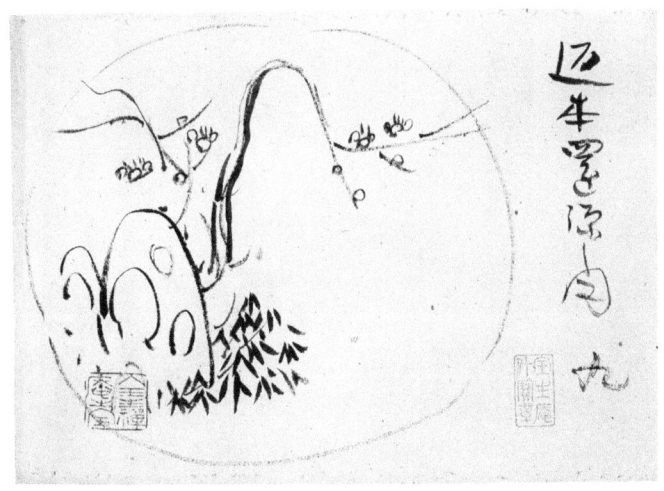

十牛図第九　返本還源牛之図

⑨ Returning to the origin, back to the source

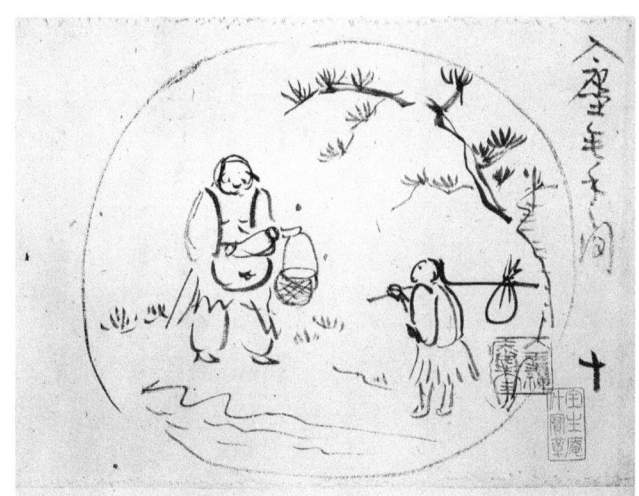

十牛図第十　入鄽垂手牛之図

⑩ Entering the city with bliss-bestowing hands

十牛図

Jūgyūzu

The 'Ten ox-herding pictures' are a representation of the ten stages of the Zen Way to enlightenment shown through pictures of an ox and its herder.

Yamaoka Tesshū (1836–1888)
Ox-herding pictures (with inscriptions in cursive script). *Sumi* ink on paper. Zenshōan collection.

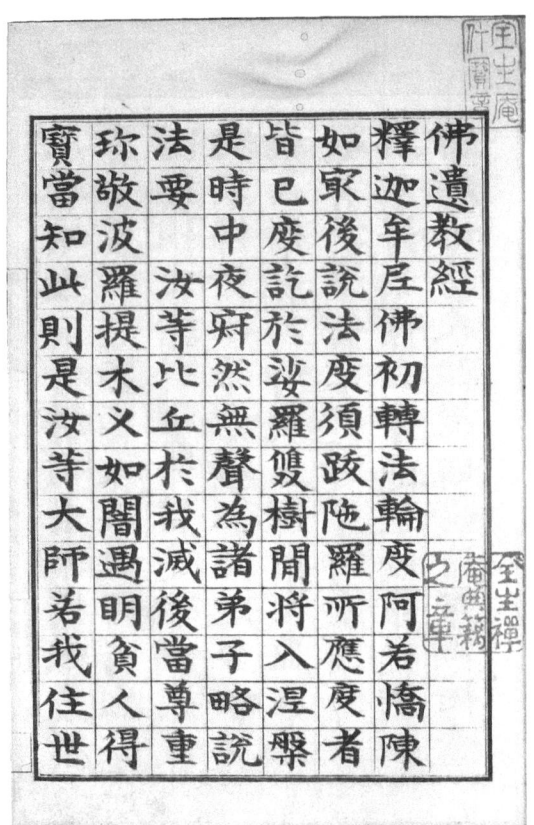
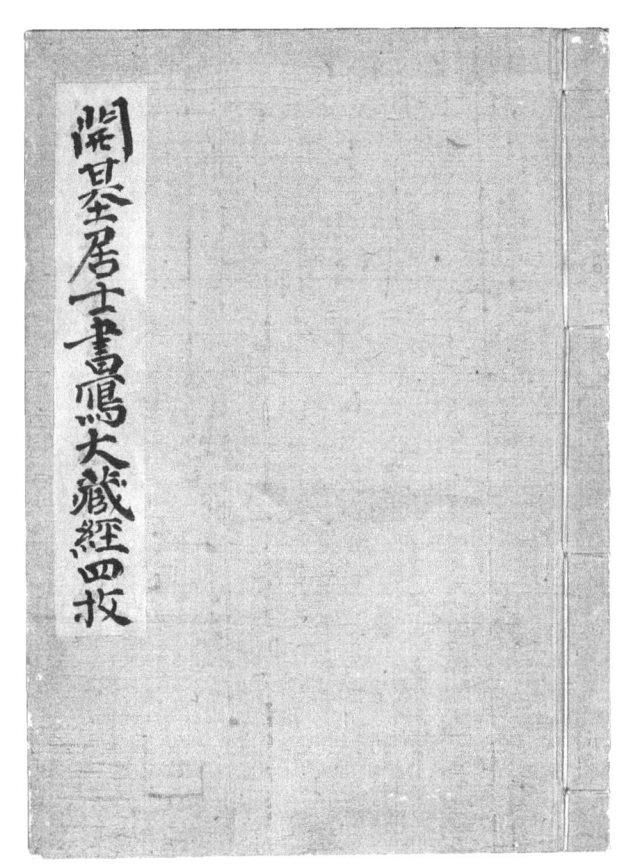

佛遺教経

Butsu yui kyō-gyō.

Sutra of the Bequeathed Teaching.

Yamaoka Tesshū (1836–1888)
Sutra of the Bequeathed Teaching (regular script). *Sumi* ink on *hanshi* size paper. Zenshōan collection.

AFTERWORD

By Takemura Eiji

The late Professor Terayama Tanchū pursued an intensive training regime of swordsmanship, Zen, and calligraphy under Ōmori Sōgen, a great master of *ken-zen-sho* who was directly affiliated with Yamaoka Tesshū (1836-88).

Tesshū was born as Ono Tetsutarō in Edo, and was the fourth son of Ono Takatomi, a retainer to the shogunate, and magistrate of the shogunate granary. He started to learn swordsmanship at the age of nine from Kusumi Kantekisai, a master of the Shinkage-ryū school, and continued to study under Inoue of the Hokushin Ittō-ryū at Hida-Takayama, where his father was appointed governor. He also became qualified in the art of calligraphy under the instruction of Iwasa Ittei at Takayama, eventually assuming the penname Ichirakusai. He began studying Zen in earnest around the age of 20.

Tesshū returned to Edo when he was 16, and in 1855 he became an assistant instructor at the shogunal military academy (Kōbusho) at the age of 19, becoming a senior instructor at 21. He also received training in the spear from Yamaoka Seizan. When Seizan met an untimely death, Tesshū married one of his sisters and took over Seizan's family name (Yamaoka).

Yamaoka became deputy statesman of the shogunate in 1867, just before the outbreak of the War of Toba-Fushimi, the initial stage of the Boshin War. In March of the same year, Tesshū was tasked with the important role of messenger/negotiator on behalf of the shogun with the leader of the imperial foces, Saigō Takamori. The sequence of Tesshū's negotiations with Saigō can be traced in an important historical document titled *Boshin kaishin-roku* (Solving of the difficult situation during the Boshin War) that is now stored in Zenshōan Temple. The document shows that after a heated discussion with Saigō, Tesshū successfully prevented a fatal clash between the shogunal and imperial armies. This led to another meeting between Saigō and Katsu Kaishū, the commander of the shogunate's army, which resulted in the peaceful transfer of power from the Tokugawa shogunate to the emperor.

Tesshū duly assumed his mission to convey the shogun's allegiance, demonstrating his strong desire for peace. It was an act that served national interests rather one that benefitted a particular lord. His ideals and actions arguably reflected the teachings of Confucianism and Confucian texts such as *Shunjū sashiden* which advocated 'autonomous judgment' and 'universalism'. Tesshū was a product of Tokugawa samurai society and education, where Confucianism was widely taught and appreciated. At the same time, the ability to pursue his difficult mission can be attributed to prolonged training in swordsmanship and Zen, which lay at the root of his personal qualities.

After the Meiji Restoration in 1868, he held a succession of important posts including the prefectural governorships of the Shizuoka Domain, Ibaragi Prefecture, and Imari Prefecture, and became an imperial retainer in 1872. For the next ten years, he served Emperor Meiji in this capacity. In 1882, he became a lifetime imperial retainer of the Emperor's Mission, and worked for the Imperial Household Agency as a close confidant of Emperor Meiji until he died at the age of 53.

The Edo period saw a substantial evolution in the techniques and philosophy of swordsmanship, and there was a massive proliferation of schools by the end of the Tokugawa regime. The Meiji Restoration and the subsequent abolition of domains (1871) jeopardised the continuation of schools of swordsmanship. One reason was because traditional martial arts were considered hopelessly old-fashioned and ineffectual in modern warfare. Another reason was that martial art schools were economically dependent on tuition fees paid by samurai. The closure of domains meant that the source of income for martial arts schools dried up. Masters of schools of swordsmanship found it difficult to survive, and many ended up selling their precious swords and books of tactics and military philosophy. These were traditionally kept strictly secret to protect the teachings of the school.

The Zenshōan is a temple in Tokyo that was founded in the Meiji period by Tesshū. It is the home for a massive collection of books and manuscripts pertaining to swordsmanship, tactics, and military philosophy. The collection includes rare manuscripts such as the great Miyamoto Musashi's *Hyōhō Sanjūgo-kajō* (35 articles on strategy). How this collection of books and manuscripts arrived at the temple remains unclear, but it suggests that Tesshū acted as a "magnet" for masters of various martial arts schools. In this sense, he was able to accumulate usually secret materials from various domains and schools of swordsmanship.

It is important to note here that Professor Terayama pursued his swordsmanship, Zen, and calligraphy in a school affiliated with Tesshū – who was a pivotal figure in the continuation and development of swordsmanship in this critical era.

Professor Terayama was arguably *the* master of *ken-zen-sho*, the art that has its roots with Miyamoto Musashi and later mastered by Yamaoka Tesshū. Another characteristic of Professor Terayama was his open-mindedness, or, more specifically, his 'universalistic' attitude; he did not seem to have any intentions to confine himself, or to remain as the master within his own school. Instead, he possessed spirited enthusiasm to exhibit the sublime nature of the art in a larger context.

His tireless efforts to share the practice of *ken-zen-sho* internationally, culminated in 'Japanese Zen Calligraphy – the Way of Zen and the Brush', the exhibition and augmenting lecture and demonstration sessions held in Oxford in 2004, and after his death in 2008. Devotedly promoted by Sarah Moate, an Oxford graduate and Terayama disciple, these events contributed to a universal appreciation for the art and for Japanese culture at this distinguished venue for academia and the arts.

It is hoped that Professor Terayama's legacy will continue.

CONTRIBUTORS

Professor Terayama Tanchū (1938-2007), was professor of calligraphy at Nishōgakusha and Sophia Universities in Tokyo, and Hanazono University in Kyoto. He practised Zen meditation and swordsmanship under Ōmori Sōgen Rōshi (1904-1994), calligraphy under Yokoyama Tenkei (1883-1966) and sword and calligraphy appreciation under Yamada Kensai (1911-1974). As part of the 1979 East-West Cultural and Spiritual Interchange Programme he organised the exhibition 'Zen and Art' in Cologne, Germany. He also acted as curator for the exhibitions 'Traces of No-Mind; Japanese Zen Calligraphy' (2001), and 'The Way of the Zen Brush – Japanese Zen Calligraphy', Christ Church Picture Gallery (2004). He was the author of numerous books on Zen and calligraphy, including *Zen and the Art of Calligraphy – the Essence of Sho*, written jointly with Ōmori Sōgen and published in English, (Penguin publications, 1983). The most recent publication in English was *Zen Brushwork: Focusing the Mind with Calligraphy and Painting* (Kodansha International, 2003, 2006). In January 2007 he was made an honorary member of the Senior Common Room of St Hugh's College, Oxford, in recognition of his scholarship and vision of the Zen arts.

(In alphabetical order)

Alex Bennett graduated from the University of Canterbury (New Zealand) in 1994, and received his doctoral degree from Kyoto University in 2001. After working as a Research Assistant at the International Research Centre for Japanese Studies until 2006, he was employed at Teikyo University's Department of Japanese Studies until 2008. He currently lectures on Japanese history and martial culture at Nagoya University of Foreign Studies, Osaka University of Health and Sport Sciences and the International Budo University. Recent publications include *Budo Perspectives* (KW Publications & Nichibunken, 2005), and *The Bushi Ethos and its Evolution: A Sociological Investigation of Bushidō* (in Japanese) (Shibunkaku, 2008).

Rupert Faulkner is Senior Curator, Japan, in the Asian Department at the Victoria and Albert Museum, where he is responsible for the collections of Japanese ceramics, contemporary crafts and *ukiyo-e* woodblock prints. His publications include *Masterpieces of Japanese Prints: Ukiyo-e from the Victoria and Albert Museum* (V&A Publications, 1991 & 1999), *Japanese Studio Crafts: Tradition and the Avant-Garde* (Laurence King, 1995), *Hiroshige Fan Prints* (V&A Publications, 2001) and *Tea: East and West* (V&A Publications, 2003). He was curator of the exhibition 'Traces of No-Mind: Japanese Zen Calligraphy' as part of Japan 2001.

Sarah Moate is a lecturer at Nihon University Faculty of Fine Arts, Tokyo. She has helped to organise three exhibitions of Japanese Zen calligraphy and painting at the Victoria and Albert Museum in London (2001 & 2008), and Christ Church Picture Gallery in Oxford (2004). She studied Zen calligraphy and the appreciation of calligraphy under Professor Terayama Tanchū. She is a Council Member of the Asiatic Society of Japan, and has recently contributed articles to *The Middle Way* (The Buddhist Society, London) and *Daihōrin*.

Takemura Eiji teaches at the School of Asia 21, Kokushikan University, Tokyo. He studied at the University of Melbourne, the University of California, Berkeley, and graduate school of SOAS, University of London. Professor Takemura was a Senior Common Room member of Pembroke College, Oxford in 2003, and SCRm (Hon.) of Christ Church in 2004. He is also a research member of International Research Centre for Japanese Studies, Kyoto, from 2002. He has published numerous works in Japanese, including works on the ethics and customs of the samurai. One of his books published in English is *The Perception of Work in Tokugawa Japan: A Study of Ishida Baigan and Ninomiya Sontoku* (University Press of America, 1997).